— Getting Started in —

Asset
Allocation

The Getting Started in Series

Getting Started in Asset Allocation by Bill Bresnan and Eric Gelb

Getting Started in Online Investing by David L. Brown and
    Kassandra Bentley

Getting Started in Stocks by Alvin D. Hall

Getting Started in Security Analysis by Peter J. Klein

Getting Start in Futures by Todd Lofton

Getting Started in Technical Analysis by Jack D. Schwager

Getting Started in Options by Michael C. Thomsett

Getting Started in Real Estate Investing by Michael C. Thomsett and
    Jean Freestone Thomsett

Getting Started in Annuities by Gordon M. Williamson

Getting Started in Bonds by Sharon Saltzgiver Wright

Coming Soon . . .

Getting Started in Mutual Funds by Alvin D. Hall

Getting Started in 401(k) Investing by Paul Katzeff

Getting Started in Financial Information by Daniel Moreau

Getting Started in
Asset
Allocation

Bill Bresnan
Eric Gelb

John Wiley & Sons, Inc.

New York • Chichester • Weinheim • Brisbane • Singapore • Toronto

This book is printed on acid-free paper. ∞

Copyright © 1999 by Bill Bresnan and Eric Gelb. All rights reserved.

Published by John Wiley & Sons, Inc.
Published simultaneously in Canada.

This publication is designed to provide accurate and authoritative information in regard to the subject matter covered. It is sold with the understanding that the publisher is not engaged in rendering professional services. If professional advice or other expert assistance is required, the services of a competent professional person should be sought.

Library of Congress Cataloging-in-Publication Data:
Bresnan, Bill, 1940–
    Getting started in asset allocation / Bill Bresnan and Eric Gelb.
      p.   cm.—(Getting started in)
    Includes index.
    ISBN 0-471-32684-4 (pbk. : alk. paper)
    1. Portfolio management. 2. Asset allocation. I. Gelb, Eric.
II. Title. III. Series.
HG4529.5.B74   1999
332.6—dc21   98-46668

Printed in the United States of America.

10 9 8 7 6 5 4 3 2 1

Acknowledgments

U nless you have taken up pencil and paper yourself, sat before that old typewriter for what seemed like ages, or spent night after night in front of the computer/word processor and written your own book, it would seem that such a project is like writing a long letter to a friend. But, it ain't so!

Even after having written several books, writing the next one still requires you to draw on a lifetime of impressions, talks, trips, people, experiences, mistakes, and all those little bits and pieces of things that resulted in you. No one writes all alone without calling on all of the above as well as the encouragement of those around you. In this case, my first acknowledgment goes to my coauthor, Eric Gelb.

Over the years, we have met, talked, read one another's works, developed a certain synergy, found a need, and combined our respective experiences, knowledge, mistakes, insight, and other bits and pieces of ourselves to produce this work. During the course of writing these chapters we have molded each other's thoughts, recast in simpler language a body of otherwise complicated material and information, and provided you, the reader, with an opportunity to look inside a segment of the financial arena that otherwise might have scared you away. Combined with the talents and direction of our editor, Debra Englander, Eric and I have been able to assemble a body of material that will prove not only useful to every investor, but informative and thought-provoking as well. I salute both of these talented people, again and again and again.

All of the people I worked with during my 22 years on Wall Street contributed more to this book than they could ever imagine. During those years, brokers, clerks, principals, and other members of the community shared their lore of the Street with me on a daily basis. While I was preparing over 20,000 candidates to take their various securities exams, I think I learned more from my students and their experiences than they learned from me. Here were fresh faces confronting Wall Street for the first time and commenting on every aspect of the business without being hampered by years of having done it every day. Theirs was a truly objective view of perhaps how it should all be done.

In addition, 4808 live financial radio shows required me to interview hundreds, nay, thousands of financial writers, analysts, fund managers, and brokers. To prepare for these interviews, I made it a point to read all of the books, articles, and other materials that the interviewee had written (being a speed reader helped a lot!). They all made a contribution to this book virtually unavailable anywhere else.

Certainly and not finally, because I pray she'll be a part of me for the rest of my life, I give thanks to my wife, Kris, for her unending encouragement and patience throughout the writing of all my books to date. We both expect that there will be many more volumes and still more hours of work to make them happen, but our love will endure all. *Jeg elsker deg*, my darling.

BILL BRESNAN

Writing a book is a tremendous and time-consuming endeavor. For these reasons, I am eternally grateful to my coauthor, Bill Bresnan. I have been a close friend and colleague of Bill since we met in 1992. It has been a pleasure to be a frequent guest on his radio shows and a privilege to collaborate and share ideas and strategies with such an esteemed professional.

To Debra Englander, our editor at John Wiley, thank you for your continuing encouragement and insights throughout the life of this work, from query to published work.

To my family: Ora, my best friend and partner, thank you for giving me so much love, support, and encouragement throughout our lives together. Thank you to my daughters, Ilana and Sara, two superstars.

Thank you to the many other people who have influenced me throughout my life. So many people have been extremely kind and generous to me. These include my teachers, coaches, supervisors, colleagues, and friends. Each one of you has had a wonderful impact on my life and in my development as a professional, a person, and a friend.

To my readers who have followed my personal finance career that spans many years: I appreciate all of your feedback and interest in my work. Thank you for continuing to read my books and articles and attend my lectures and presentations. Best wishes for every success.

ERIC GELB

Contents

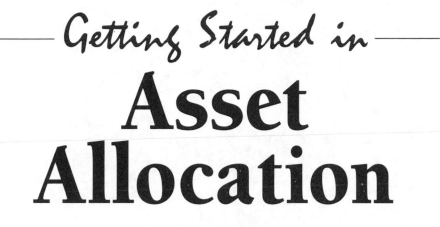

Getting Started in

Asset Allocation

Splitting Your Investment Pie

T his book is a practical book for helping you enjoy a better life. In other words, this book explains how you can put your financial plan into action to achieve your financial goals and objectives. For you this may mean buying a new or a larger home, buying a boat, enjoying a comfortable retirement, and funding your children's or grandchildren's college education. In large part the key to achieving your financial objectives is discipline and asset allocation.

Asset allocation is a common buzzword heard in conversations about finance. Business journalists and talk show hosts routinely discuss allocation. A number of financial planners say allocate 100 percent of your *assets* to common stocks and that's it. Despite all the commentary and analysis, there is still a fair degree of skepticism and mystery surrounding the subject. This book is designed to help you comprehend the concepts behind and importance of asset allocation and apply asset allocation in your life.

> **assets** things/property owned. Your assets would include your home, car, stocks, bonds, collectibles, and so on, while your business might own machinery, equipment, and land.

Asset allocation means dividing your money into investment baskets, each with the objective of achieving a specific blended or overall

return on your portfolio. When you split your money among different asset types, you should be able to smooth out the value of your investment
portfolio as well as the rate of return. The theory behind asset allocation is
that different asset types or classes perform differently at different times.
In other words, when one asset type increases in value, another asset type
may decline in value. This is called *correlation.* Asset allocation is designed to help you avoid the devastating effect of a stock market crash or
prolonged bear market.

return   reward on an investment. Return can be
expressed in a number of ways in the world of money:
the dividends received on a stock owned, interest on a
bond, the satisfaction of stability in your portfolio, and
a combination of dividends or interest with appreciation
to produce total return.

correlation   the relationship between two or more
different securities held in a portfolio where one rises in
value when the other falls or one goes up in value and
the other goes up as well. A well-balanced portfolio
would have assets allocated to make this happen during
active markets.

Suppose an investor puts all of his or her money into common
stocks. Then, the portfolio returns would be 100 percent based on the
success or failure of common stocks. If the stock market rises in value as
it has done over the past 16 years, the returns would be strong. If, on the
other hand, the stock market crashes or experiences a prolonged bear
market, and the value of stocks declines by 60 percent, the investor would
lose 60 percent of the value of his or her portfolio. Asset allocation is designed to help you pick the optimal mix of investments for you and your
circumstances and minimize downside risk while smoothing out the
value of your portfolio and your returns over the long run.

Asset allocation is extremely important to your investment health
and financial well-being. Asset allocation means investing your money
across different classes of investments or types of assets. Perhaps you

might put a portion of your investments in common stocks and a portion in *bonds, money market instruments*, and real estate. A large portion of the rate of return on your investments is determined by the types of investments or asset classes you select and their relative percentage in your portfolio.

bonds   evidence of an obligation to repay in the form of promissory notes or IOUs usually issued by a corporation, municipality, government or government agency to the holder. Bonds usually run for 10 or more years to maturity.

money market instruments   short-term securities or deposits that mature within a period of 270 days to one year.

In the ideal, the goal of asset allocation is to help you capture the highest returns for the least amount of risk. Over the long run, the returns on common stocks have exceeded the returns on bonds and money market instruments. But in the short run, the values and returns on common stocks have tended to fluctuate widely. By investing a percentage of your money (investment portfolio) in common stocks, bonds, money market instruments, real estate, and other types of investments, you should be able to create a more steady portfolio with a smoother return profile.

Asset allocation helps you avoid *market timing*. Market timing is the technique of buying and selling investments at the precise point in time you expect an asset class to move up or down in value. Numerous studies have shown that market timing does not work. It is nearly impossible to pick the exact day or week when an asset class is about to take off. Similarly, other studies have shown that the most successful investors and wealth builders pursue a consistent and disciplined investment strategy over the long run. Asset allocation and this book can help you accomplish those goals and become a more successful investor.

Asset allocation provides a framework for the long run. Once you select an allocation (channel a certain percentage of your assets into each investment category), you can follow that framework over the long run. Of course, you must monitor the results of your portfolio. You may want to adjust your asset allocation periodically to bring your portfolio back into line with your target allocation. You may want to adjust your allocation to reflect changes in your financial position, life stage, and financial objectives.

> **market timing**   using various indexes that measure the state of the economy, interest rates, or other variables to make buy and sell decisions (e.g., you expect interest rates to drop because of certain seasonal factors, etc., so you purchase fixed-income securities whose value will rise as interest rates fall).

Nonetheless, an asset allocation plan offers you the guidelines and system to create a steady investment process and program and optimize your wealth over the long run. The key is the long run because you want to manage your money over your lifetime. This means investing when you are young to build wealth so you can live a better life during your working career and your retirement. This requires a system of procedures. That saving and investment system or program can take on a number of forms, such as automatic payroll deductions and automatic investments into a savings program, dividend reinvestment program (DRIP), or mutual fund directly from your checking account.

Asset allocation is not a new concept. Asset allocation is based on the fundamentals of budgeting. In other words, when you budget your money, you divide or allocate your money across various spending categories such as rent, food, savings, entertainment, and medical. If you are a movie buff, you have probably seen *I Remember Mamma*. In the film, the family sits around the dining room table and divides or allocates their money into categories. Irene Dunne, who plays Mamma, says, "For the grocer" or "for the landlord" as she places a few coins into various envelopes.

This book is written for the person who is looking to establish a disciplined investment program and implement a financial plan. We address risk and *reward* and asset allocation techniques. Model investment portfolios are explained and illustrated. Asset types are discussed and analyzed from the perspective of whether they fit your particular goals and objectives rather than analyzing the quality of each investment. Individual investment selection is not the subject of this book.

reward the benefits you received in exchange for what you paid or what action you took. Perhaps you purchased shares of common stock and the price rose; your reward is the realized gain. Or, you bought a bond and received interest; your reward is the interest income.

To determine how to optimize your investment returns, this book helps you through the six-step process of evaluation.

1. *Understanding the terminology and techniques of asset allocation.* The terminology of asset allocation is relatively straightforward. Nonetheless, it is important to understand the buzzwords to gain an understanding of how to use asset allocation to your benefit. By gaining a command of asset allocation techniques, you can learn the power of asset allocation regarding managing your investment portfolio.

2. *Understanding risk and how asset allocation can reduce or increase your investment and portfolio risk.* In other words, all investments carry some degree of risk. Common stocks can experience wide fluctuations in price during the short run, but long-term returns have been relatively consistent and strong. Treasury bills have been relatively stable and consistent; however, the income is subject to U.S. federal income taxes and inflation. Treasury bill investments are susceptible to the risk that you will lose the purchasing power of your money over time through inflation.

3. *Managing your money over your lifetime.* Money management is a lifetime process where you are likely to invest when you are in the workforce, and invest and harvest or spend your money when you retire. When you are young, in theory, you should be able to assume more risk than when you are older. You'll want to establish an asset allocation that takes your individual profile into account. As your financial position and circumstances change, you may want to assume less risk over time and adjust your asset allocation accordingly.

4. *Understanding the psychology of investing and asset allocation.* To some extent investing and asset allocation is more art than science. Recently, we met with a retired couple in their early 70s.

The couple, while they had been married to each other for over 40 years, had different *risk tolerances* and different perspectives on how to manage their money. The husband wanted to adopt a more conservative approach and allocate the lion's share of their portfolio to fixed-income investments. The wife wanted to assume more risk and invest a greater percentage of their money in common stocks. The couple was split over psychology and attitude and the reality that they were retired. They were no longer members of the workforce and they had a relatively long life expectancy. They were faced with the issue of managing their money over the remainder of their lifetimes in light of inflation and not earning additional income to invest (other than dividends, interest, and capital gains).

risk tolerance   how much of anything owned you are prepared to lose. Can you tolerate the loss of 25 percent of your assets and still be able to feel comfortable? Or, are you a person who cannot bear to see $1 of your portfolio lost? Somewhere between that first dollar and all you have will be a true expression of your individual risk tolerance level. No two people have the same ability to tolerate risk.

5. *Managing your money and establishing a suitable asset allocation in light of your investment goals and objectives.* Asset allocation is a tool designed to help you implement your financial plan in a disciplined way to achieve your financial goals. If you want to achieve higher investment returns, it is likely you will have to assume greater risk. This typically means investing in common stocks and other riskier asset classes. If you have a longer time horizon, investing in common stocks may prove to be a wise investment decision and the volatility of your portfolio is likely to be reduced over time. If you have a longer time horizon, you can elect to save and invest more money and the power of compound returns helps your cause. Given a longer investment horizon, you may be able to establish a more conservative asset allocation and tilt your asset allocation in favor of lower-risk assets. We will examine all these points throughout this book.

6. *Evaluating asset classes and investment types with respect to your financial plan.* Once you establish an asset allocation, you can evaluate investments with respect to whether they would enhance or diminish your overall portfolio and expected investment returns.

Asset allocation, like any other investment strategy and tool, must be appropriate and suitable for the individual. This book presents a framework for selecting an asset allocation for the individual. No one idea, model portfolio, or system works for every investor, and asset allocation is no exception to this rule. Asset allocation as an investment and portfolio management tool can be extremely valuable in the process of choosing investments to help you achieve your investment goals and objectives. But remember, selecting an investment program and asset allocation can be a lot different in practice than in theory. It is important to select asset classes and investments based on your specific circumstances, financial position, tolerance for risk, and level of sophistication. This book is not designed to be a substitute for working with a financial planner or investment adviser.

You will have the best chance of financial success by becoming an informed investor. This entails establishing financial goals and objectives and determining how much wealth you would like to amass. This also means making a realistic assessment of how much money you have and how much money you are in a position to invest and yes, even lose. Of course, you must determine your risk tolerance and level of sophistication as well. By considering all these factors, you should be in a better position to establish the optimal asset allocation and investment program for you. Building wealth is the combination of becoming an educated consumer of financial products, selecting quality investments, and establishing a disciplined program for the long run.

Asset Allocation Explained

ASSET ALLOCATION DEFINED

Asset allocation means dividing your investment portfolio and investable dollars into different asset classes. The theory behind *asset allocation* is that by splitting your investment portfolio into different types of investments, you can reduce the *volatility* of the value and returns of your portfolio. In other words, asset allocation can help you smooth out your portfolio value and overall return on investment.

asset allocation   division of assets to accomplish personal goals based on age, financial time horizons, financial position, personal risk tolerance, family needs, years to retirement, and so on.

volatility   the rise or fall of a market, stock, or bond in a particular period of time. Highly volatile stocks are suitable for only those investors with a higher risk tolerance level.

Your asset allocation program should be the combination and culmination of your individual goals, financial timetable (time horizon), risk tolerance, and investment objectives. These factors and their relative importance to you will help you determine just what percentage of your investment portfolio you want to place at more or less risk, in longer- or shorter-term investments, and even in taxable or-tax free investments. One person's asset allocation model is likely to be different from another person's program. No two asset allocation models are likely to have a large percentage of their assets in the same asset class, aimed at the same goals and objectives, or at the same level of risk.

THE PIZZA PIE ANALOGY

Perhaps the easiest way to begin to describe asset allocation would be to visualize a pizza pie. Imagine that a round pizza pie represents your investment portfolio. Most people cut a pizza pie into eight equal slices. If you follow this model exactly, you would divide or allocate your investment portfolio into eight equal parts. You might put one-eighth (100 percent divided by 8, or 12.5 percent) of your investment portfolio into common stocks and one-eighth of your investment portfolio into bonds, and so forth. This allocation may or may not be a realistic asset allocation for you.

ASSET ALLOCATION ON A PRACTICAL BASIS

Few, if any, of us lead such simple financial lives and have such simple goals and objectives as to be able to neatly fit our investment portfolio into eight equal portions or slices. Each asset allocation will be different based on the individual's or couple's goals and objectives, risk tolerance, and financial position. These topics are discussed in this chapter and in Chapter 2.

Each individual or couple must establish lifestyle objectives and investment goals and objectives and then design a specific and personal asset allocation. Simply putting X percentage of your investments into one asset class with a particular investment objective and investing Y percentage of your dollars in another asset class with a particular investment objective will not necessarily create a properly allocated portfolio. As you will learn in future chapters, you must establish investment goals and objectives and then determine the percentages of your investment portfolio to invest in each asset category.

Your asset allocation must clearly reflect *your* goals, address *your* objectives, fit *your* investment and life cycle timetable, and otherwise do only what *you* need to do and get done with *your* money. Asset allocation is very personal and will be ineffective if you fail to design *your* asset allocation program to meet *your* needs.

To maximize your wealth and develop an asset allocation program that will yield the most value to you and your family, learn the concepts explained in this book and follow the action steps to develop your own personal asset allocation model.

SELF-EXAMINATION

Before you can begin to divide your investment capital into slices appropriately, you must complete a great deal of self-examination. Keeping in mind that asset allocation is a personal endeavor and an evolving process, each person will have different goals and objectives and different financial circumstances, all changing over time.

FINANCIAL GOALS AND OBJECTIVES

First, consider your financial objectives. In other words, what would you like to accomplish in your lifetime? Everyone has unique and individual personal goals and objectives. You may want to live on a tropical island in the Caribbean and play golf twice a day; you may want to live on a boat and sail the seven seas; perhaps you want to donate your money to your alma mater, church or synagogue, hospital, or other nonprofit organization; you may want to educate all your grandchildren through grad school; or maybe you'd just as soon spend all of your money during your lifetime. You see, your financial objectives are just that: *yours*.

Here are a few common financial goals:

✔ Buy a home.
✔ Buy a new car.
✔ Buy a boat.
✔ Build a swimming pool.
✔ Take a vacation every year.
✔ Travel to exotic locations.
✔ Establish an emergency fund.
✔ Start your own business.

✔ Fund your children's college education.

✔ Fund your children's weddings.

✔ Build enough wealth to retire comfortably.

✔ Build enough wealth to retire early.

Don't be ashamed, embarrassed, or even concerned about what anyone, including your own personal financial professional, thinks about your financial objectives. What you want from your money is your choice and it's your adviser's job to show you how to accomplish those goals based on the assets and income available, as well as your personality. Setting your financial objectives and goals should be about as selfish as making out your own will. The only consideration is you and your wishes. Obviously, your objectives should be realistic in the sense of whether they can be achieved; otherwise this will be a fruitless exercise.

As you decide which life cycle phase you are in and which phase you want to plan for, read Chapters 9 through 14. In each chapter, we profile people at a different stage in life. We apply asset allocation to financial objectives relevant to that group.

If you are single, financial planning and asset allocation may be a relatively straightforward exercise. When your financial plan includes a spouse or partner, and you may face the responsibility of caring for others such as children, parents, and grandparents, planning becomes much more complicated and involved. Typically, in these cases you will need more financial resources and discipline to accomplish your financial goals and objectives.

TUG-OF-WAR

When you plan your financial future with a spouse or partner, the two of you must conduct lengthy, candid, and in-depth dialogue. As a first step, each partner should analyze his or her own preferences, biases, goals and objectives, and anxieties. Then both of you, individually, should commit to paper your thoughts in those areas.

These discussions can become heated and sometimes upsetting, especially since proper financial planning entails considering your personal fabric and personality. With most topics, and especially money, people cling to their personal goals and feelings. Sometimes, these discussions can become contentious. To the best extent possible, it is important to maintain a reasonable perspective and try to focus on the fact that your collective purpose is to advance your family and your well-being together. In some cases, we have recommended that couples divide their resources.

Each partner would have a personal allocation for a portion of their investment assets and they would have a common plan and allocation for the remainder of their investment assets. Generally, it is more efficient, economical, and positive for family members to pool their resources and work toward common and shared goals and objectives.

ASSET ALLOCATION FACTORS

To create the optimal asset allocation program, you must consider a number of factors and components. In the preceding section, we discussed personal goals and objectives. To a large extent, financial goals and objectives are the overriding force in determining an asset allocation. In effect, the more ambitious and costly your personal goals, the more money you have to accumulate in order to realize those goals and objectives. For example, if you would like to retire and be in a position to spend $100,000 per year, that is a more ambitious goal than wanting to be in a position to spend $50,000 per year. The former goal requires more money and therefore a longer investment (wealth accumulation) horizon, greater savings and investment earlier on and probably over time, and perhaps more aggressive (risky) investing.

In other words, to achieve higher financial goals, you will probably have to strive to earn higher investment returns. This translates into allocating your assets more heavily into riskier asset classes such as common stocks.

However, other factors are significant with respect to creating your asset allocation program:

- ✔ Age.
- ✔ Life expectancy.
- ✔ Financial milestones.
- ✔ Responsibilities and financial obligations.
- ✔ Time horizon.
- ✔ More aggressive investing.
- ✔ Conservative approach.
- ✔ Financial position.
- ✔ Income sources.
- ✔ Expected market returns.
- ✔ Risk tolerance.

Age

Your own age, your spouse's or partner's age, and the ages of your children (and any others who rely on you for financial support) are very important factors in financial planning and asset allocation. The younger you are, the more time you have available to take advantage of the power of compound returns, the greater your risk tolerance, and the more ability you have to recover from financial mistakes and losses.

Life Expectancy

You should visit your doctors to determine your life expectancy and study your family history. You should gain a sense of your life expectancy and any hereditary diseases or conditions you may face. Once you assign a financial cost to any ailments, you can estimate your likely financial needs. As appropriate, you can alter your financial plan to prepare for these possibilities.

Financial Milestones

Earlier in this chapter, we listed financial goals, including buying a boat or building a swimming pool, funding your children's education, funding your children's weddings, and retiring. The best way to achieve your financial goals is to assign a specific date to each goal. Then tailor your portfolio and asset allocation to meet these goals.

Suppose you want to retire when you reach 55 years of age and that is 14 years from now. In order to reach your goal, you have to allocate your assets to build enough wealth to fund your retirement years, which would be likely to span 25 to 30 years (with a life expectancy of 80 to 85 years). In the coming decades, you will probably have to plan for a retirement that may be longer than your total working life. Assuming you are 41 years of age and continue working up to age 55, you will earn a paycheck for the next 14 years and must dedicate a certain amount of your current income to build your retirement assets.

You can handle any goal in this fashion.

Responsibilities and Financial Obligations

Your personal responsibilities and financial obligations will play an important role in determining how much money you have to invest and how you should allocate your assets. More and more families are becoming multigenerational households. For example, parents, grandparents, aunts, and uncles in their 60s, 70s, 80s, and, as we move on into the next century, still-healthy relatives in their 90s and 100s may live with you. And let's be sure to consider that ever-growing phenomenon of your grown children alone or with their entire nuclear family returning to the nest, but who still need your care and financial support.

Time Horizon

In the previous few paragraphs, we discussed the time horizon between now and when you want to realize your goal. In the retirement example, there are at least two time horizons mentioned. The first is that the person wants to retire in 14 years. This has implications about how much money this person needs to save and invest in order to achieve the desired retirement lifestyle. The second is that the person expects to live for 25 to 30 years in retirement. This implies that the money has to last at least 25 to 30 years (this ignores how much money the retiree would like to leave heirs).

The longer your time horizon to accumulate wealth, the more time you have to build enough wealth to achieve your goals. Suppose you begin saving and investing money today; the longer your time horizon, the less money you have to invest now to achieve your financial goal. Suppose you have an opportunity to make one lump sum investment today that yields 8 percent forever, and you want to accumulate $1 million in 40 years. Table 1.1 illustrates the power of compound returns. It shows the lump sum investment you need to make today in order to accumulate

TABLE 1.1 Compound Returns and Time Horizon—8 Percent Return	
Years until Goal	Investment Needed Today
40	$ 46,031
35	67,635
30	93,777
25	146,018
20	214,548
10	463,193

Note: This example assumes that you pay income taxes from another source of funds.

$1 million, assuming an investment yield of 8 percent for the entire time horizon (investment period). Notice from the table that if you want to accumulate $1 million in 40 years, you have to invest $46,031 today. If your time horizon is only 10 years, your required investment increases to $463,193, a sizable difference.

The point of the example and the following two examples is that the longer your time horizon, the less money you need to invest today to achieve your financial goal.

More Aggressive Investing

If you could assume more risk and make an investment that earns a 10 percent rate of return, you could make a smaller lump sum investment. (See Table 1.2.) For the 40-year time horizon, the $46,031 investment drops to $22,095. For the 10-year time horizon, the $463,193 lump sum investment drops to $385,543, still an enormous sum of money.

Table 1.2 illustrates the lump sum investment you need to make today in order to accumulate $1 million, assuming an investment yield of 10 percent for the entire time horizon (investment period). Notice from the table that if you want to accumulate $1 million in 40 years, you have to invest $22,095 today. If your time horizon is only 10 years, your required investment increases to $385,543.

Generally, to achieve higher returns, you have to assume incrementally higher degrees of risk. Depending on your personal circum-

TABLE 1.2 Compound Returns and Time Horizon—10 Percent Return	
Years until Goal	Investment Needed Today
40	$ 22,095
35	35,584
30	57,309
25	92,296
20	148,644
10	385,543

Note: This example assumes that you pay income taxes from another sources.

stances and situation, you may or may not want to undertake this additional risk.

Conservative Approach

Alternatively, you could adopt a more conservative approach. Suppose that you expect to achieve the 8 percent rate of return. However, you want to hedge your bets and ensure that you achieve your financial goal—accumulate $1 million in 40 years. You decide to assume that you will earn only a 7 percent rate of return. Accordingly, at a 7 percent rate of return, to accumulate $1 million in 40 years, you should invest $66,780 today. (See Table 1.3.) You can use a financial calculator or computer spreadsheet program that computes present and future values to help you calculate investment amounts. Or, work with your accountant, financial planner, or investment adviser.

Table 1.3 illustrates the lump sum investment you need to make today in order to accumulate $1 million, assuming an investment yield of 7 percent for the entire time horizon (investment period). Notice from the table that if you want to accumulate $1 million in 40 years, you have to invest $66,780 today. If your time horizon is only 10 years, your required investment increases to $508,349.

Alternatively, you could make the lump sum investment today and make additional lump sum investments in years two, three, four, and so on. This way, you will have more money working for you and you are

TABLE 1.3 Compound Returns and Time Horizon— 7 Percent Return	
Years until Goal	*Investment Needed Today*
40	$ 66,780
35	93,663
30	131,367
25	184,249
20	258,419
10	508,349

Note: This example assumes that you pay income taxes from another sources.

more likely to achieve your financial goals. This also provides you with a cushion in case you do not realize your expected returns.

Financial Position

Your financial position also plays a major part in determining your asset allocation. To the extent you have accumulated significant wealth, it should be easier for you to achieve your financial goals. To the extent you earn a relatively high current income, it should also be easier for you to achieve your financial goals. Of course, this depends on your spending habits and cost structure. In general, the more money you have and the higher your income, the more likely you are to achieve your financial goals. Of course you have to invest your money wisely.

Income Sources

In discussing financial position we raised the point that the higher your income, the more financial power you have to invest more money and re-alize your financial goals. Regarding retirement planning and setting financial goals, we already considered the wealth you will accumulate. Several other points to consider are your pension, Social Security, and any inheritances you may receive.

Social Security and pension payments are designed to provide additional income to you during your retirement. As with all investments, it is important to analyze the creditworthiness of the payer. In other words, how likely is it that these sources will be in a financial position to meet their payment obligations?

The press mentions that the U.S. government is taking steps to save the Social Security program and ensure that future generations will receive payments. To the extent you rely on Social Security, your financial health depends on the financial strength and health of the Social Security system. You should monitor the Social Security Administration's financial condition and plan your own saving and investment program accordingly.

Similarly, your employer or your union may be responsible for paying your pension benefits when you retire. You'll want to monitor the financial health of these parties and plan your finances accordingly.

Expected Market Returns

Earlier in this chapter, we discussed the effect of different rates of return on an investment or on your investment portfolio (see Tables 1.1, 1.2, and 1.3). If you assume that your investment portfolio will yield 10 percent and you invest accordingly, and your actual returns equal only 7 percent or 8 percent, your wealth will be less than you expected. You may fall short of your financial goals.

Similarly, the long-term (1926 to 1997) rate of return on the S&P 500 index of common stocks has been 11 percent per annum. (Used with permission. © 1998 Ibbotson Associates, Inc. All rights reserved.) By comparison, the rate of return on the S&P 500 index of common stocks has been 37.43 percent in 1995, 33.36 percent in 1996, and 23.07 percent in 1997. (Used with permission. © 1998 Ibbotson Associates, Inc. All rights reserved.) These current returns substantially exceed the long-term average rate of return. Therefore, it is reasonable to assume that future returns will revert to the long-term mean (average) and be less than 25 percent to 30 percent per annum. Make sure you invest enough money over time to ensure that you achieve your financial goals in light of actual market returns that may be less than your expected returns.

Risk Tolerance

Your tolerance to assume risk will play a large factor in how you allocate your assets. In Table 1.2, we considered an investment that yields 10 percent rather than the initial 8 percent rate of return. In general, the 10 percent investment inherently bears more risk than the 8 percent investment. Two ways to view risk are as volatility and probability of losing money. In other words, the 10 percent investment is likely to be more volatile than the 8 percent one: The investment value will fluctuate up and down more widely. Most likely, the 10 percent investment carries a higher probability that you will lose some or all of your investment than the 8 percent investment.

> Over the long run, based on past performance, the stock market has posted the highest returns among stocks, bonds, and money market investments. As you might expect, the common stock asset class bears the highest risk or volatility of these three categories. Your tolerance for risk will help you determine whether you want to allocate more of your investment portfolio toward the 8 percent, 10 percent, or 7 percent categories.
>
> If you don't like volatility and risk, you may want to gravitate towards the 8 percent and 7 percent yielding (lower-risk) assets than the 10 percent yielding assets. This implies that the conservative person's asset allocation will be different from the aggressive person's asset allocation.

HOW TO SPLIT YOUR INVESTMENT PIE

Every person reading this book, at one time or another, may have commuted to work either by car or public transportation, flown in an airplane, ridden on an elevator, or bought a lottery ticket. In each of these examples, you took some risk. But, the real question is . . . when you assumed those risks, did you know, in your heart of hearts, that you could have sustained an injury or lost all the money you placed on the line?

We all have 100 percent risk tolerance as it applies to some of our money. The question is how much of our money are we comfortable placing at complete and total risk. While every investment, action, and inaction contains some degree of risk, the key is to analyze those risks and allocate our investment portfolio accordingly. Allocate only those dollars you are ready to lose to the highest-risk investments and work your way down the risk ladder with the rest of your investment portfolio.

Just what percentage of those dollars you have worked a lifetime to accumulate and feel comfortable placing at high risk is a personal and individual decision. Perhaps you should look into the mirror and ask yourself, "How many of those dollars am I ready to lose?" When you analyze yourself and your tolerance for risk, you will gain a new and more practical appreciation for risk. We all have a certain level of risk tolerance; it's just a matter of knowing what our level really is.

Since risk is such an important aspect of asset allocation, please study Chapters 2, 5, 6, and 7 for a more in-depth discussion of the various kinds of risk inherent to each category of investment. You must understand the nature and characteristics of every investment you make before you invest your money.

ALLOCATION VERSUS DIVERSIFICATION

Asset allocation is those boxes or baskets in which we make certain investments. In other words, asset allocation means how we divide up our investment portfolio across different asset classes or investment types.

Diversification means purchasing a number of investments or securities within an asset category or class in order to reduce investment or *unsystematic risk* (this is explained further in Chapter 2).

Suppose John, an individual investor, decides to allocate 15 percent of his investment portfolio to generate tax-free income (we discuss tax-exempt municipal bonds (munis) in Chapter 6 in more detail). John's portfolios net worth equals $1 million, so 15 percent equates to

$150,000. The 15 percent or $150,000 represents the percentage of John's portfolio he allocates toward investing that generates tax-exempt or tax-free income.

diversification   spreading your assets among different securities (growth, income, etc.) or different quality securities (within an asset class or mutual fund) for the purpose of spreading out your risk. The opposite of diversification would be having all your eggs in one basket.

unsystematic risk   risk from competition or obsolescence rather than from market forces or "interest rates." *See* **systematic risk.**

Within that 15 percent allocation or basket, John might own:

✔ $50,000 in AAA-rated general obligation bonds.
✔ $50,000 in A-rated revenue bonds.
✔ $25,000 in Baa-rated bonds of a small municipality.
✔ $25,000 in nonrated bonds (junk bonds) of an even smaller community.

In this example, John allocated $150,000 of his investment portfolio toward his personal investment objective of generating tax-exempt income. Within that category, he diversified his investments among bonds issued by different municipalities and selected bonds of different maturities. This sort of diversification, within the asset allocation model, accomplishes the goal of reducing unsystematic or specific investment risk.

The maturities selected would match the average maximum yield available at the time you invest, based on the then current yield curve. For example, yield may peak in five to six years before flattening or even declining. Those maturities would produce the best yields available at that time.

As you will note from the individual components of this model portfolio, there is consideration given to risk tolerance as well. Each of the bonds listed bears a different credit rating and some are safer than others.

Some are higher- or lower-rated bonds; some are from larger or smaller issuers, and one issue is highly risky as indicated by the fact that the security is nonrated. A closer look might even reveal bonds with different maturity dates (addressing that personal financial timetable we discussed earlier); some of the bonds might pay interest at different times of the year and some might also be tax-exempt federally and at the individual state level as well.

Were no consideration given to diversification, we would simply have bought $150,000 in face value from a single issuer, with a single maturity date, all paying interest in the same months and all equally rated by Moody's Investors Service or Standard & Poor's, two nationally recognized credit rating agencies.

Asset allocation coupled with proper diversification can mean the difference between meeting your goals and objectives and missing the mark. Placing your portfolio at greater risk than you can tolerate may result in your losing sleep and not having enough money available to meet your personal financial timetable. Similarly, assuming too little risk may result in your losing too great a percentage of your wealth to inflation, and this may mean you fall short of your financial goals.

WHY ASSET ALLOCATION IS ADVANTAGEOUS

In this chapter, we explained the concepts and nature of asset allocation. We have provided examples in order to illustrate the mechanics of asset allocation. To summarize, here are the four major benefits and advantages to asset allocation:

1. By establishing your own personal asset allocation, you can develop and implement your own financial plan to suit your needs and personality.
2. Proper asset allocation means making a financial plan and examining the following factors to achieve the optimal portfolio composition and risk-return trade-offs. Once again, the key consideration in an effective asset allocation program is *you*:

   ✔ Your financial timetable.

   ✔ Your personal financial objectives and goals.

   ✔ Your financial position.

   ✔ Your risk tolerance level.

✔ Your ability to understand the investments recommended.

✔ Your estate concerns.

✔ Your tax bracket and estate tax considerations.

3. A disciplined approach to investing and managing your money and a well-thought-out and developed asset allocation program should take a lot of the guesswork out of investing money.

    A quick look at the over 8000 mutual funds existing today will clearly show that there are an infinite number of investment choices and types of investment vehicles. By establishing an asset allocation program or portfolio blueprint, you will be well ahead of the game regarding which types of investments and mutual funds you should select for your investment portfolio.

4. Asset allocation combined with prudent diversification will help you to smooth out the volatility of your investment portfolio and smooth out your overall rate of return. In other words, these two strategies used together should help you to increase your return while taking on less risk.

Chapter

Risk

A sset allocation is a risk-return management technique that investors can use to maximize investment return (reward) for assuming a certain amount of risk. We can use asset allocation to:

✔ Review the overall risk inherent in our investment portfolio and make changes to our portfolio—buy or sell investments.

✔ Determine whether we are over- or underweighted in a particular investment or asset class.

✔ Gauge whether we need to assume more or less risk in order to achieve our financial goals.

✔ Determine whether a new investment under consideration or a current investment we are monitoring will help or detract from our target asset allocation.

Before we discuss asset allocation, we should examine risk and what risk means. *Risk* is the uncertainty or probability of achieving or not achieving a certain outcome or expected rate of return. Some risks are inconsequential. Investors can manage many risks by selecting certain investments and avoiding other investments (portfolio selection and asset allocation). Other risks are unavoidable.

risk   the uncertainty or probability of achieving or not achieving a certain outcome or expected rate of return.

THE NATURE OF RISK

If we stop to consider everyday life, we can observe risks high and low. Some risks, like catching a common cold, are likely to occur (high probability). At the same time, other risks, such as catching a more serious disease, are relatively unlikely to occur (low probability). In the case of the common cold, for most people the probability of catching a cold in the winter is relatively high. But the consequence or cost of catching a cold is relatively low—high probability, low cost. Therefore, there is relatively low risk involved. We can analyze and manage investment risk in much the same way.

RISK VERSUS VOLATILITY

Risk is the variability of returns on investment. When investors purchase *U.S. Treasury bills (T-bills)* that mature in a year or less, they take relative comfort in the fact that the instrument has a stated or known face value at *maturity*, it matures in a relatively short period of time, and the interest rate or *yield* is known. Most important, the T-bill is backed by the *full faith and credit* of the U.S. government. The rates of return on common stocks, bonds, or mutual funds comprised of common stocks or bonds as well as most other classes of investments typically do not offer the same relatively stable return as a U.S. Treasury bill.

U.S. Treasury bills (T-bills)   Treasury securities that mature in periods up to one year.

maturity   the date the face amount of a debt security comes due and must be paid by the borrower. At maturity, the holder of a bond is owed the full face value of that bond regardless of market conditions. Some debt instruments mature in 10, 20, or even 30 years from their date of issue.

yield typically the return earned on a debt security. A $10,000 bond with a 5 percent coupon is said to have a nominal or stated yield of 5 percent or $500 per year. As the market price of that bond goes up or down the current yield moves in the opposite direction.

full faith and credit usually applies to the bond or debt market and means that no specific asset stands behind that debt, but rather the borrower's full faith and credit. In the world of government debt that backing represents the government's ability to print money (tax the people).

Risk also encompasses buying an investment that is overpriced in relation to its *intrinsic value* and the investment's inherent risk. When you purchase a common stock where the market price of the stock equates to a *price-earnings ratio (P/E ratio)* of 40, the investment community (Wall Street) has placed relatively high expectations on the company's ability to generate future growth in revenue and *earnings per share (EPS)*. In the event the company fails to meet Wall Street's earnings expectations, portfolio managers are likely to sell the stock. Heavy selling typically drives down the price of the stock. In such cases, the market price of the common stock may be too high—higher than the stock's intrinsic value. We see that today, particularly when a growth stock's actual quarterly earnings fail to meet Wall Street's expectations.

intrinsic value the value of that which makes up what you own. The intrinsic value of a gold coin would be the current market price of gold times the weight of the coin in question. In the world of options, the intrinsic value of the option would be the difference between the market price of the stock and the strike price. If you own a call with a strike price of $45 and the stock is selling at $47, the intrinsic value of the option is $2. Out-of-the-money options and options trading at-the-money have no intrinsic value.

price-earnings ratio (P/E) reflection of the number times the earnings per share the stock is selling at. If a company shows earnings of $2.50 per share and the market price is 27½, the stock is selling at a P/E of 11 or is worth 11 times the earnings of $2.50 per share. Historically a P/E of below 20 has been considered conservative and a P/E above 20 has been considered more speculative.

earnings per share (EPS) a company's earnings for the last period (quarter or year) divided by the weighted average number of shares outstanding for the period.

On the other hand, perhaps another company's common stock is trading at market price that equates to a P/E of 11 or 12. This relatively low P/E reflects Wall Street's lower expectations for this company's future prospects than the company with the 40 P/E ratio. To the extent the company with the low P/E ratio (or the high P/E company) delivers earnings growth that exceeds Wall Street's expectations, the market price of the stock is likely to rise. In this case, the intrinsic value of the stock would be higher than the market price.

Volatility means the swings or changes in the price or *market value* of an investment. In the case of the Treasury bill, since the investment is viewed to be relatively stable and the instrument matures in a relatively short period of time, the volatility or price movements are likely to be relatively small. Common stocks, long-term bonds, and other investments that have either a relatively long time horizon or a less certain outcome (more risky), are likely to be more volatile. The market prices of these investments are likely to experience greater movement or variability over time, especially in the short run.

market value the current value of a security. If you owned a share of ABC Company common stock and the bid price of the stock was $72, you could sell that share of stock for $72 minus sales commissions.

TEN TYPES OF RISK

To adequately manage risk, it is important to develop a framework for analyzing risk. Here are 10 types of risk investors typically face:

1. Liquidity risk.
2. Market risk.
3. Investment risk.
4. Inflation risk.
5. Interest rate risk.
6. Currency risk.
7. Credit and repayment risk.
8. Structural risk.
9. Reinvestment risk.
10. "Do nothing" risk.

Liquidity Risk

Liquidity risk is the difficulty investors face when they sell their investments and want to recover cash. Consider an investor who purchases a *penny stock*. The *float* or number of shares of common stock traded at any one time is likely to be relatively small. One or perhaps two *market makers* or specialists make a market in the stock. This security or issue is called a thinly traded stock. In such cases, the market cannot absorb major sales or purchases without significant changes in the market price of the investment.

> **penny stock**   any stock selling at $5 or less per share. Penny stocks are usually stocks of new companies with little or no financial history or trading track record and for the most part are for those investors with a high risk tolerance. Sometimes called cats and dogs.

It can be very discouraging to own 5000 shares of a common stock with an *unrealized gain* only to learn that when you want to sell your investment, the market will absorb only 500 shares at the current *bid* price. To unload the rest of your shares, you could sell successive shares at lower and lower prices. The final total proceeds may result in a *realized gain* that is less than your expected (unrealized) gain.

float   the number of shares issued by a corporation that is in the hands of the shareholders as opposed to the total number of shares that that entity could otherwise ultimately issue (sometimes referred to as the public float); the outstanding and tradable shares. In the banking community the term applies to the time period between the writing of a check and its actual clearing at the bank upon which it was written.

market maker   a broker-dealer firm that buys and sells securities for its own account. This firm stands ready to buy securities (make a bid) and sell securities (make an offer) in particular companies they either like or may have been active in bringing public. This activity is performed by a specialist on the floors of the various exchanges.

unrealized gain   a gain in an asset that has not been taken by selling the asset off. You bought a stock at $50 and it is now worth $60. You have an unrealized gain in that holding of $10 and no tax is due until and if you sell. *See* **paper profit.**

bid   the price at which an investor can sell an investment to the market maker.

Direct ownership of real estate is another example of a form of liquidity risk due to the time needed to convert the investment into cash. With real property, the sales process can span months. The real estate broker's commission typically runs 6 percent of the sales price of the property. This is similar to the bid and *ask* spread associated with the purchase and sale of a security. The sales price may vary between the time you list (offer) the property for sale and the time you close the sale. Liquidity risk can be especially significant when you are likely to need your money (cash) on short notice.

> **realized gain**   the difference between the purchase price and the higher selling price of a security that has been taken by selling the asset. A realized gain is a taxable event, as opposed to an unrealized gain or a paper profit.

> **ask**   the price at which you can buy an investment from the market maker.

Investors can manage liquidity risk through asset allocation by managing the percentage of your portfolio that you allocate to illiquid investments.

Market Risk

Market risk is the risk that outside factors affect the market prices of your investment portfolio. Examples of types of market risk include changes in *interest* rates, recessions, new regulations, and changes in consumer prices. These macro factors affect the market at large and may cause wide swings in the value of your investment portfolio. Macro factors influence companies and therefore the market prices of securities in varying degrees and in different ways. As a result, to some extent investors can reduce the impact of market risk by using asset allocation techniques to select different classes of investments. Market risk is also called *systematic risk*.

Investment Risk

Investment risk is the risk that an outside factor will affect a particular company or industry, but not the market at large. Examples of investment risk include business risk, competitive risk, management risk, and technological obsolescence. Investment risk is also called unsystematic risk.

interest   paid to the lender by the borrower, this is the cost of using money. The most common form of interest is the amount you pay the bank to borrow the money used to purchase your house. This is known as mortgage interest and is generally paid on a monthly basis along with a part of the principal. If you lend money to a corporation or government by buying their bonds, they pay you a semiannual amount for the use of that money and then repay the principal upon the maturity of that bond, frequently as long as 20 or 30 years out.

systematic risk   beyond the future prospects of the company itself to produce earnings, sell products, and become profitable, there exists market risk and interest rate risk. The company owned may do well internally, but interest rate changes and a falling stock market may bring its price down in spite of those profits.

One example of investment risk is a long distance telephone carrier that faces competition from an Internet provider. Another example is a postal system that faces competition from overnight delivery services, facsimile machines, long distance telephone carriers, or the Internet. To a large extent, we can manage investment risk through asset allocation.

Inflation Risk

Inflation is the loss of purchasing power due to the increase in the prices of goods and services. Inflation particularly affects fixed dollar payments. Suppose you invest in a bond that pays an annual *coupon* of $100. Assuming the issuer (borrower) does not default on its obligations under the indenture to pay interest and principal on the bond, you will receive interest income of $100 every year until the bond matures. Over time, as the prices of goods increase and the coupon on the bond remains constant at $100 per annum, your purchasing power declines. You are able to buy less and less with that $100 *fixed income*. The long-term inflation rate is considered to be approximately 3 percent. This means one dollar today is worth only 97 cents in one year.

inflation the loss of purchasing power due to increased prices. As the prices of food, fuel, and housing rise, more dollars are required to purchase those goods and services.

coupon piece of paper attached to a bond that represents the semiannual interest due to the bondholder. A typical 30-year coupon bond would have 60 coupons representing the semiannual interest payments for the next 30 years or the remaining life of the bond. When the coupon is detached and sent to the bank named, the bondholder receives a check for six months of the interest due.

fixed income the semiannual interest paid by a government or corporation to its bondholders. This amount, expressed in dollars, remains fixed even if the market price of the bond fluctuates in response to market conditions.

Consider a bond that pays a 6 percent coupon. This equates to a $60 annual interest payment on a $1000 bond. Generally, interest income is subject to income taxes; let's assume the income tax rate equals 30 percent. When an investor recognizes $60 in interest income and pays income taxes at 30 percent, the investor pays $18 in income taxes ($60 in income multiplied by 30 percent tax rate). Interest income after income taxes equals $42 ($60 minus $18). Inflation claims 3 percent of this amount in the first year, or $1.26. Real interest income after taxes and after inflation in the first year equals approximately $40. Inflation takes a bigger chunk out of our purchasing power (it compounds) every year.

Businesses that have the power to grow their operations and raise the prices of their goods and services can often increase their revenues and profits in excess of the inflation rate, and perhaps increase their quarterly *dividend* payments. These types of investments can include common stocks, real estate investment trusts (REITs), and utilities. Also, the newly created inflation-indexed U.S. Treasury bonds offer protection from inflation.

> **dividend** payout by a corporation to its preferred and common shareholders of moneys from earnings. Dividend payments usually occur on a quarterly or semiannual basis out of already taxed dollars.

Investors can manage a certain amount of their exposure to inflation through asset allocation. To some extent, investors can select companies that benefit from the declining cost of high technology.

Interest Rate Risk

Interest rate risk is the change in value of an investment that arises from a change in market interest rates. Changes in interest rates particularly affect the prices of fixed-income securities (notes, bonds, etc.). With fixed-income investments, the price of the investment moves in the opposite direction of (inversely to) interest rates.

Market interest rates tend to move based on investors' expectations about the rate of inflation. When investors perceive that inflation will fall, market interest rates tend to fall and the prices of fixed-income securities tend to rise. Another factor that may cause market interest rates to move is when the Federal Reserve Board (the Fed) changes the *discount rate* or adjusts the *margin requirement*. These moves may cause lenders to increase or reduce their lending rates and change the amount of money they make available for loans.

> **discount rate** the rate of interest the Federal Reserve Bank charges member banks to borrow against their own reserves. An increase in the discount rate is said to signal a period of tight money, and a drop in the discount rate by the Fed would indicate easy money. Such moves are usually followed by an increase or drop in the member banks' lending rates.

Suppose you purchase a bond with a coupon of 6 percent that matures in 10 years. You purchase the bond at *par* or $1000. Every semiannual period, assuming the borrower is not in default, you receive a $30 ($1000 multiplied by 6 percent divided by one-half year) coupon (interest payment). Suppose that the market interest rate increases to 8 percent. Now, the same borrower who issued the 6 percent coupon bond (and other borrowers of similar credit quality) would issue bonds at par ($1000) with an 8 percent coupon. The 8 percent or $80 coupon matches the current market yield.

margin requirements   also known as margin rate; the amount you can borrow from the brokerage house to purchase securities. The current margin rate is 50 percent of the purchase price on applicable stocks. When the Federal Reserve Board raises the requirement it is tightening money, and when it lowers the requirement it is easing the money supply.

par   the face value of a bond, traditionally $1000.

When market yields equal 8 percent, a bond that pays an 8 percent coupon should have a market price of $1000 or par. The same investor would consider buying the 6 percent bond that pays a $30 semiannual coupon for less than $1000. Since he or she could invest $1000 and purchase a new bond that pays a $40 semiannual coupon, the investor would pay less than $1000 for a bond that pays only 6 percent. Actually, the market price of the 6 percent bond would drop to reflect the change in market yield. In effect, the market price of the 6 percent bond would drop to $864.10 such that the 6 percent bond's *yield to maturity (YTM)* equaled 8 percent.

The reverse is also true. In the event market interest rates fall, the market price of existing bonds (and other fixed-income securities) will rise so the investment's yield to maturity equals the current market yield.

Common stocks and other investments are affected by changes in market interest rates in varying degrees. Certain common stocks, especially real estate investment trusts (REITs) and utilities that pay relatively high dividends, often behave like fixed-income investments; they are relatively sensitive to changes in market interest rates. Generally, the longer the time to maturity and the lower the coupon rate, the more sensitive the market price of the investment is to changes in market interest rates.

yield to maturity (YTM)   the average return on a bond between the date of purchase and the date the bond matures. This calculation takes into account the fixed interest paid every year as well as the gain or loss realized by holding the bond to maturity. Generally speaking, a bond bought at a discount and held to maturity has a YTM higher than the nominal or stated yield because a gain in value is realized along with the interest income (and vice versa for a bond bought at a premium.)

Investors can manage interest rate risk to a large extent through asset allocation. Investors can also invest a portion of their money in short-term fixed-income securities or money market instruments that tend to pay floating interest rates. Investors can implement a strategy called a bond *ladder*. This entails purchasing bonds of different maturities: bonds that mature in one year, two years, three, four, five, and so on. Every year some of the bonds mature and you can reinvest the principal in new bonds with longer maturities.

ladder   staggering the maturities of debt instruments to obtain an average return (e.g., investing $100,000 in U.S. Treasury bonds by buying $20,000 pieces maturing at, say, two-year intervals going forward).

Currency Risk

Currency risk is the gain or loss arising from changes in the relative value of foreign currencies. On a given day, one dollar may be the equivalent of 130 yen. On another day, one dollar may buy 125 or 140 yen. Depending on the exchange rate, one yen converts into more or less than one dollar. Suppose a U.S. company has business operations in Japan and sells goods and services in Japan. The company's sales revenue is likely to be denominated in yen. When the company exchanges the yen-denominated revenue into U.S. dollars, the exchange rate may change and the company will realize more or fewer dollars.

A manufacturing plant located in Asia may experience an increase or decrease in labor costs as a result of currency changes in that country. Suppliers may raise or lower the cost of the components they are making available for a given product as the value of their own currency moves. This factor can impact the companies in other countries depending on the relative prices of goods and services.

Let's consider the example of foreign bonds that pay coupons or foreign stocks that pay dividends. On January 1, a U.S. investor buys a German government bond that pays a 6 percent coupon. One U.S. dollar equals 170 deutsche marks (DM). To buy a DM 1000 bond, the U.S. investor pays $5.88. During the year the German government pays 6 percent or DM 60. When the U.S. investor converts the coupon that is denominated in deutsche marks into U.S. dollars, suppose that $1 equals 150 DM. The coupon converts into $0.40. Suppose that the exchange rate moves where $1 equals 200 DM. Now, the coupon converts into $0.30. In the event that the exchange rate moves where $1 equals 125 DM, the DM coupon converts into US $0.48. The investor faces currency risk when the bond matures and the investor wants to convert the principal that is denominated in deutsche marks back into U.S. dollars or into another currency.

Investors can hedge currency risk through the futures market or through asset allocation to a large extent.

Credit and Repayment Risk

Credit and repayment risk means the likelihood the borrower or issuer will not pay your coupon or dividend on the *payable date* or repay your principal on the due date. In some ways, credit and repayment risk is more important with respect to fixed-income investments (bonds, notes, etc.) than *equity* investments. Moody's Investors Service and Standard & Poor's Corporation rate the creditworthiness of borrowers. These rating agencies may rate an entity AAA or another similar rating that is the highest credit rating. The higher the credit quality of the issuer, the higher the company's credit rating and the more likely it is to repay its debt. In the event the business faces financial difficulties, the credit quality of the borrower may deteriorate and the bondholders may risk losing a portion of their investment.

payable date   the date on which a coupon or dividend is payable to an investor.

equity stock representing ownership rather than a bond representing a debt owed by the corporation to the bondholders. Equity is also the difference between the value of something owned and the debt owed against it. If you own a $250,000 home with a $150,000 mortgage, your equity in that asset is the difference, or $100,000.

Municipalities' and governments' credit ratings are tied to their *tax base*. Perhaps a neighborhood deteriorates and businesses leave. The municipality's tax revenues are likely to decline and the municipality's credit quality declines as well. *General obligation (G.O.) bonds* are backed by the full faith and taxing power of the municipality or local government that issues the bonds. These *municipal bonds* are typically viewed as carrying the highest credit rating of the municipality or governmental entity. *Revenue bonds* or special project bonds are typically backed by the money collected from a particular project or business. Two examples are tolls from bridges or fares from buses and subways. The credit quality of these types of bonds varies based on the nature, importance, strength, predictability, and profitability of the project. The more stable the project, the higher the credit rating of the bonds.

tax base in the world of muni bonds, the tax base represents those entities in a community whose property taxes would pay the interest and ultimately the principal on bonds issued by the town, city, or political subdivision in question. A large residential or business population paying substantial taxes to a city makes it possible for that city to issue considerable amounts of debt, service that debt, and, because of the large tax base, pay a lower rate of interest to borrow those moneys.

Investors typically pay more attention to credit and repayment risk when they analyze fixed-income investments; however, equity investors also face repayment risk. Many common stockholders expect to receive quarterly dividends. To the extent the company has issued preferred stock and the board of directors does not declare the stated dividends on the preferred stock, the directors are precluded from paying dividends on the common stock. With cumulative preferred stock, all preferred stock dividends due and unpaid must be paid before the company can declare a dividend to the common stockholders. At some point, the common stockholders expect to recover their initial investment or realize any appreciation in the stock price.

general obligation (G.O.) bonds   obligations backed by the borrower's full faith and credit. General obligation municipal bonds are those backed by the issuer's taxing authority, as opposed to revenue bonds, which depend on the revenues generated by the project financed, like a toll road or a bridge.

municipal bonds (munis)   bonds issued by cities, communities, towns, or other political entities (in effect, moneys borrowed by the people of the community) for projects related to that community. Munis are often used to finance schools, hospitals, toll roads, tunnels, sewers, or fire equipment, and the interest paid is free from federal taxation. If the muni is owned by a resident of the city that issued it, that resident's income from such a bond could be triple tax-free—exempt from federal, state, and city income taxes.

revenue bond   a type of municipal bond that is backed by the revenue income from the project financed rather than the taxing authority of the issuer. Revenue bonds are frequently issued to pay for toll roads (backed by the tolls) and sewer installations (backed by sewer hookup charges).

With foreign bonds or stocks, the companies that owe these related payment streams may experience financial difficulty. The governments where these companies are based may prohibit cash (currency) from leaving the country. Then, the investors face repayment risk. This is often called political or sovereign risk.

Investors can use asset allocation to vary the credit quality of their fixed-income investments.

Structural Risk

Structural risk is the risk investors face from changes in the marketplace and the structure of investments. Futures and options, or *derivatives*, have created structural risk in the marketplace. A derivative is a financial instrument that derives its value from the value of the underlying security. A *call* option on ABC Company common stock derives its value from the price of a share of ABC Company common stock, the option's *strike price*, and the time until expiration. Derivatives are generally more highly leveraged than the underlying issues themselves. So, the value of a derivative is likely to be more volatile than the value of the underlying security itself. Futures, on the other hand, represent a play on the future value (compared to today's value) of commodities such as grains, meats, and precious metals, rather than stocks.

derivatives securities that are created using other securities or parts thereof. They derive their value from the success or failure of the underlying security and not from sales, profits, or other activities. Examples are DIAMONDS and "spiders," basically trusts whose value is based on the rise and fall of the value of the 30 components of the Dow Jones Industrial Average and the S&P 500 Index, respectively.

call a type of option giving the owner the right to purchase a security from the grantor (the seller of the option) at a fixed price (the exercise price) for a predetermined period of time. Calls are usually purchased in anticipation of a rising market.

strike price   the exercise price of an option. If you own a call with a strike price of $50 and the stock is selling at $60, you can exercise the call (buying the stock at $50) and sell the stock into the open market at $60. The strike price is fixed and remains the same for the life of the option.

Suppose you own a derivative and are a holder of the underlying shares of common stock. A drop in the value of the call option derivative is likely to bring down the value of your holdings as well. However, such a drop in the value of the derivative is likely to be magnified by several times compared to the underlying shares due to the highly leveraged nature of derivatives.

One of the best ways to offset the effect of structural risk is to *hedge* your position in the futures or options market to the extent of your original investment. If you own a bond, for example, you could hedge your position by purchasing or selling an interest rate future. If you own common equities or equity mutual funds, you might hedge your position with Standard & Poor's 500 Index futures or even "spiders" (SPDRs®—Standard & Poor's Depositary Receipts®) that are traded on the American Stock Exchange (AMEX). With most investments, it is possible to establish a hedge or offsetting position to protect you against adverse market conditions.

hedge   a strategy employed when you want to offset one or more types of investment risk using another investment vehicle. You feel that the market price of a particular stock you own may go down in the future and you want to protect those gains already realized. You could purchase a put option and lock in the price at which you could sell (put the stock to the grantor of that option) during the next three months.

Investors can use asset allocation to manage the composition of their portfolio.

Reinvestment Risk

Reinvestment risk is the risk that you will be unable to reinvest your coupon payments or dividends at an investment rate that is equal to or greater than the coupon or dividend rate earned initially. Reinvestment risk has the greatest impact on fixed-income investments such as bonds. Suppose you invest in a bond that pays a 12 percent coupon. You receive coupons totaling $120 every year until the bond matures. In the event market interest rates (reinvestment rates) drop below 12 percent, it is unlikely you will be able to reinvest your 12 percent coupon in a new investment that yields 12 percent. Your overall internal rate of return or yield will be less than 12 percent.

One way to minimize reinvestment risk is to purchase zero coupon bonds. These bonds pay no current coupons, so the yield to maturity equals the return on investment. Another way to manage reinvestment risk is to utilize a bond ladder. This entails purchasing bonds of varying maturities. As one bond matures, you invest in another one that matures at least one year after the longest maturity in your portfolio.

Investors can manage reinvestment risk through asset allocation.

Do-Nothing Risk

Do-nothing risk is the risk of waiting for the proper moment to invest your money. Another way to look at this is called market timing. Do-nothing risk is often the most overlooked risk of all the risks investors face. Think of yourself waiting for the stock market to move in a particular direction. Consider that it is human nature being what it is that is causing you to stay on the sidelines while you wait for the markets to settle down or simply move to your target level. Missing the market is probably one of the biggest mistakes average investors make time and time again.

One investment rule to follow is: Budget your money so you invest on a regular basis. Invest whenever you have money available under the prevailing market conditions, and be ready to adjust those investments when the market changes or your financial circumstances change.

RISK-REWARD TRADE-OFF

Risk-reward or return trade-off is the return that compensates an investor for assuming risk. Typically, investors demand higher compensation or returns for assuming more risk. The T-bill may yield approximately 3 percent while a corporate bond may yield approximately 5 percent. High-yield or *junk bonds* may yield 10 percent to reflect the lower credit quality (higher credit risk) of the borrower.

> **junk bonds**   bonds issued by companies with either a very short financial track record or a very poor credit rating and credit history. Having a Standard & Poor's or Moody's credit rating of BB⁺ or lower, they would not be considered investment-grade.

Wall Street considers T-bills to be risk-free investments since they are backed by the full faith and credit of the U.S. government. As investors move along the risk spectrum and make riskier investments, they expect higher returns. If T-bills yield 3 percent, corporate bonds yield 5 percent, and junk bonds yield 10 percent, then the expected return on common stocks should be at least 10 percent.

Investors can manage their risk-return profile through asset allocation and selecting investments that offer a fair or higher than expected return for the risk they expect to assume.

DETERMINING YOUR RISK TOLERANCE

Risk tolerance means a person's ability and level of comfort in taking on (assuming) a given level of risk. Different people have different tolerances for assuming risk. Some people get thrills from visiting a casino and betting on the roll of the dice at the craps table, from playing the horses, or from playing roulette. Some of these people routinely make $100, $1,000, or $10,000 wagers. When they lose money, they may bet another $100 or $1,000 to recover their initial investment. They may double down and bet $200 or $2,000 to earn double the profit. In these circumstances, perhaps dampness forms on the palm of your hands. Maybe your stomach begins to churn. Your body is telling you that you have reached the limits of your ability to withstand (assume) risk.

Risk tolerance varies across people and varies over time. Younger people typically have more time (years) to recover from investment losses and career mistakes than older people. Wealthier people generally have more power to recover from investment losses because they can earn more money or have a greater net worth. The key is to assess your personal situation, circumstances, and tolerance for risk and then plan an investment strategy accordingly.

You can determine your risk tolerance by analyzing your personality and lifestyle. Pull out a piece of paper or notebook and make a list of your personality attributes.

✔ Age.

✔ Career status (i.e., whether you have eached your highest earnings potential).

✔ Stage in life (i.e., beginning your career, retiring, retired, saving for a home or college).

✔ Socioeconomic level (rich, poor, etc.).

✔ Annual income (fixed salary, bonus, commission, overtime, etc.).

✔ Net worth (your wealth).

✔ Lifetime income prospects.

✔ Financial obligations (i.e., supporting a family, paying off a *mortgage*, etc.).

mortgage the amount of money borrowed to purchase a home. Sometimes, the money borrowed (margined) to purchase securities; a first mortgage bond would be one backed by a lien on a specific piece of real property owned by the borrower/issuer.

Generally, the older you are, the more established you are in your life, and the more financial obligations you face, the lower your risk tolerance. A recent college graduate in his or her 20s who intends to work for the next 35 to 40 years is likely to have a much greater ability to recover from investment losses and career setbacks than an older person. Retirees in their 60s and 70s are probably trying to conserve their money and live out their retirement years as comfortably as possible. The retired person most likely has the least ability to recover from investment setbacks. Risk tolerance varies by person and also varies over time.

PROBABILITY OF RISK AND MATERIALITY

Earlier in this chapter, we discussed the risk and probability of catching a common cold. The risk of catching a cold is most likely relatively low and the probability of catching a cold is relatively high. Since the consequence or cost of catching a cold is relatively low, there is low risk. Risks that have a low probability or likelihood of occurrence and that have a low cost or consequence if they occur are generally immaterial. Investors can use asset allocation techniques to manage risk and analyze the materiality of risk.

RISK OF FAILING TO ATTAIN FINANCIAL GOALS

Risk of failing to attain your financial goals typically occurs because of two factors. First, you fail to make a financial plan and fail to make adequate investments, so you find yourself short on funds to carry out your dreams. (We assume that this does not apply to you since you are reading this book.) Second, you make a financial mistake or your investments do not yield the hoped-for returns.

Depending on how important your goals are, failing to reach your goals will have lesser or greater consequences. If you currently own a car and want to buy a new one but have not saved enough money, you may postpone the purchase. If your car breaks down, though, you may be disappointed or inconvenienced if you cannot buy that new car on schedule. Then, failing to attain your financial goals has consequences.

If you want to retire and you have not accumulated sufficient wealth, this can have serious consequences, especially if you become infirm or incapacitated. You may have to postpone your retirement, live a less comfortable retirement, or continue working during your retirement.

The risk of failing to attain your financial goals has greater consequences as the importance of the goal increases. You can manage this risk by planning ahead, managing your spending, saving enough money, investing money every month, and investing wisely.

CONCLUSION

Risk is inherent in all investment portfolios. But, you can use asset allocation techniques to manage your risk. Once you become a good consumer of financial products, you should be able make wiser investment decisions. In the next chapter we discuss reward or return on investment.

Chapter 3

Reward

In this chapter, we discuss the concept of reward. Reward comes in many shapes and sizes. The reality is that we all want the greatest reward while assuming the least amount of risk. It would be wonderful to receive $1 million today, with no strings attached and no risk whatsoever. Unfortunately, this is unrealistic. In other words, to be in a position to reap higher returns or rewards, generally we need to take on more risk. This risk-reward trade-off is particularly the case with investments.

WHAT IS REWARD?

Reward means the benefit from taking a particular course of action. Most people think of reward as a monetary payment—dollars. But reward can be emotional as well: peace of mind—comfort that you will sleep well at night—or satisfaction that you have attained a certain level of wealth.

Here are a few types of rewards that may interest you:

- ✔ When you were a youngster, your mother promising you candy if you behaved for the day.
- ✔ In western movies, the sheriff offering a cash reward of $1000 for information leading to the capture of the bad guy.
- ✔ Giving your teacher an apple in hopes of getting a better grade.
- ✔ Buying a lottery ticket and hoping that the numbers you chose won and you receive $10 million.

In each of these cases, someone took specific action with the expectation or hope of receiving a benefit or reward. Making investments of any kind is really no different from these examples.

Here are a few of the more common financial rewards that may be important to you:

- ✔ Buy a stock and receive a dividend every quarter.
- ✔ Hold a stock for some period of time where the price of the stock rises (capital gain).
- ✔ Own a corporate, government, or municipal bond (fixed-income security) and collect interest every six months.
- ✔ Buy those same bonds at less than face value (at a discount) and hold them to maturity when you *redeem* them for face value (at par or $1000).
- ✔ Experience a drop in market interest rates while holding those bonds, where the market value of the bonds increase.
- ✔ Purchase a collectible and watch its resale value increase in connection with supply and demand and inflation.
- ✔ Purchase a collectible and, although its market value stays the same, hang it on the wall and enjoy it.
- ✔ Fund your child's or grandchild's education for the personal satisfaction of doing so.
- ✔ Take comfort in the fact that your portfolio mix and asset allocation make you confident that you are assuming the right combination of risk and return for you, so you can sleep well at night.

redeem   to turn in for payment at maturity. If you bought a bond a number of years ago and that bond matured this year, you would return the bond to the issuer for payment of the face value. Upon redemption, you could now reinvest the proceeds elsewhere.

It is very important to establish your financial plan and asset allocation in light of your investment and financial objectives and risk tolerance. Reward may mean accumulating a certain amount of wealth, but achieving that objective may mean that you have to assume a great degree of risk—perhaps more risk than makes you feel comfortable. As you follow this book and determine your personal asset allocation, it is important to consider which rewards you seek and what levels and types of risk you are willing to assume.

EXPECTED RETURN BY CATEGORY

Each asset class or category is characterized by an expected rate of return. The greater the amount of effort we put into something, the greater the reward we expect to receive. If we work more hours than our coworker, we will receive a larger paycheck at the end of the week. If we spend more time mastering our job and trying to advance our career, either through advanced education or more technical training, we should command a higher salary and position than our coworker who did not put in quite so much effort.

In general, when we speak of investments, the more reward we expect to receive, the more risk we have to assume to attain that reward. Other considerations must be kept in mind as well. Just because you commit more money to a particular investment than someone else does not necessarily mean that your reward will automatically be greater. The key is to analyze the risk-reward trade-off inherent in each investment, establish the overall risk-reward trade-off inherent in your portfolio, and decide whether this level is suitable for you. You can accomplish the latter through asset allocation.

The following table lists the rates of return by category for different asset classes. (Also see Figure 3.1.) The data reflects long-term rates of return for the period 1926 to 1997*:

Category	Rate of Return
Small-cap common stocks	12.7%
S&P 500—large-cap common stocks	11.0
Long-term corporate bonds	5.7
U.S. Treasury bills	3.8
Inflation	(3.1)

Generally speaking, the greater the possible reward, the greater the chance that you will lose most or all of your investment. Consider penny stocks (stocks that sell for under $5 per share and are usually issued by start-up companies with little or no track record or financial history). Many of you may have bought a stock at under $1 per share only to see it

*Used with permission. ©1998 Ibbotson Associates, Inc. All rights reserved.

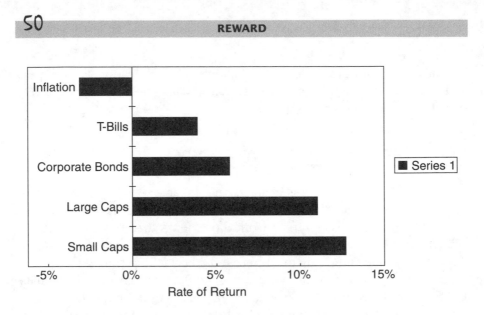

FIGURE 3.1 Annual total returns by category.
Used with permission. © 1998 Ibbotson Associates, Inc. All rights reserved.
Certain portions of this work were derived from copyrighted works of Roger
G. Ibbotson and Rex Sinquefeld.

trading at several dollars in just a few days. Some of you, ourselves included, have bought stocks for less than $0.25 and seen them go to $6,
$8, $10, or more, perhaps in a relatively short period of time.

However, we have made other similar investments only to see the
value of those penny stocks fall. In reality, the companies lacked real substance and the price of the stock was driven up to $6, $8, or $10 because
of artificially developed investor demand rather than business substance
or financial success of the enterprise.

To put reward into perspective, consider that the potential for reward increases as the relative safety of the principal decreases. In other
words, the more risk you assume, the higher your expected reward. Of
course, when you seek the highest reward, you run the greatest risk of losing your initial investment.

Similarly, when we purchase a U.S. Treasury bill, we expect the highest relative level of safety. The investment matures within a relatively
short period of time, often 91 days. We expect the U.S. government to repay our principal plus interest. In exchange for this relative safety, we expect little or no volatility in the value of the investment and we expect no
risk to our principal and interest income. With this investment, we buy
safety (low risk) in exchange for low return.

We have separated the following asset types into groups based on the relative risk of each investment. In other words, high-risk assets offer potentially high rewards and the greatest volatility. Also note that we consider each risk as it relates to different asset classes in Chapters 5, 6, and 7. Regardless of the risk and reward associated with these asset classes or groups, it is always important that you understand the nature of the investments you are considering and the investments currently in your portfolio.

High-Risk Assets

✔ Commodities/futures trading.
✔ Exploratory oil and gas funds.
✔ Managed commodity funds.
✔ Research and development projects.
✔ Stock options (buying them or selling naked stock options).
✔ Developmental oil and gas drilling programs (raw land/vacant lots).

Medium-Risk Assets

✔ Leveraged equipment leasing deals.
✔ Individual stock accounts.
✔ Real estate development programs.
✔ Investment-grade rare coins.
✔ Highly leveraged real estate.
✔ Investment-grade precious gems.
✔ Oil and gas income programs.
✔ Growth mutual funds.
✔ Low-leverage real estate (for income and growth).
✔ Income equipment leasing programs.
✔ Blue-chip income securities.
✔ Municipal bonds.
✔ High-grade corporate bond funds.
✔ Triple net leased real estate (all cash).

Low-Risk Assets

✔ Single-premium deferred fixed annuities.
✔ Municipal bond funds.

✔ Long-term government bonds.

✔ Personal residence (your own home/vacation home).

✔ Certificates of deposit (CD's).

✔ Money market certificates.

✔ Treasury notes and bills.

✔ Money market mutual funds.

✔ Cash, gold, and/or silver (in your safe-deposit box).

✔ Cash value of life Insurance policies.

✔ Passbook savings accounts.

✔ Series EE and HH U.S. savings bonds.

INCOME, DIVIDENDS, AND CAPITAL APPRECIATION

The primary reason we invest our money is for reward—to live a better life tomorrow than today. The primary form of reward or return on investment is money. When most investors think of reward, they make a mental trade-off between the risk they assume today compared to the reward they expect to receive tomorrow. The most common types of rewards associated with investments are: income, dividends, and capital appreciation.

Income

Income is a key form of reward. Most investors consider current periodic income to be a relatively stable and consistent form of reward. For example:

✔ Fixed-income securities such as notes and bonds pay semiannual interest income.

✔ Money market instruments such as certificates of deposit (CDs) and commercial paper pay periodic interest income.

✔ Blue-chip stocks typically pay quarterly dividends.

✔ Real estate that is leased to creditworthy tenants for 15 years is likely to provide a relatively reliable income stream.

You will determine your need for current steady cash income depending on your life stage and financial position, and establish your asset allocation accordingly. As you get older and most likely adopt a more conservative investment approach and asset allocation, you will be likely to emphasize relatively lower-risk assets in your portfolio and a greater percentage of investments that pay current and reliable income. Especially when you retire, current cash income can be of greater importance to pay your living expenses.

Generally speaking, unless you need to receive more spendable dollars from your portfolio or need your principal for a certain spending objective within a relatively short time frame, you can find greater potential for higher returns elsewhere. If you are in retirement and no longer a member of the workforce or have that desire or need to receive more spendable dollars, you should allocate a greater portion of your portfolio toward income-producing investments.

You can calculate how much spendable income you need or desire by preparing a simple personal budget. Once you determine your total spending needs, consider your sources of income and cash.

The Internal Revenue Service (IRS) considers all of the following items to be income although you may not consider many of these categories as income investments:

- ✔ Your salary.
- ✔ Pension income.
- ✔ Retirement plan distributions.
- ✔ Social Security benefits.
- ✔ Self-employment income.
- ✔ Interest earned.
- ✔ Dividends.
- ✔ Capital gains from sale of securities and other capital property.
- ✔ Gains from the sale of your house.
- ✔ Forgiveness of debt you owe someone else (you are relieved of your obligation to pay).
- ✔ Royalties.
- ✔ Barter income.
- ✔ Rental of personal property.
- ✔ Estate and trust income.
- ✔ Director's fees.
- ✔ Gambling winnings (including lotteries).

These items are forms of income. Your income is the primary force that fuels your spending and investment.

In particular, the IRS considers these items to be income, and will tax you accordingly. But for the purposes of this book, we will limit our discussion to investment income and asset allocation. We suggest that you review the IRS's Publication 17 as well as its other free tax publications (available directly from the IRS by mail or by calling 1-800-829-3676, or through participating post offices and libraries). These publications reveal all of the income categories, beyond investment income, that the IRS lists. As a general rule, if someone else is deducting the amount paid, the amount is taxable income to you.

To realize more current cash income from your investment portfolio, allocate more of your portfolio assets into fixed-income investments and into common stocks that pay dividends.

Assuming you seek a 5 percent to 7 percent rate of return, you can calculate that for every $10,000 you invest for income, your return should equal $500 to $700 per year. We address inflation and asset allocation and spending the principal component of your portfolio in Chapters 1, 4, 8, 10, 11, 12, 13, and 14.

Dividends

Dividends are periodic payments that represent a distribution of a company's earnings. A company's board of directors will declare a dividend on common and preferred stocks. For example, a preferred stock may pay you a $2.50 dividend every quarter. Perhaps you own 100 shares of common stock of the Coca-Cola Company and the company declares a $0.15 per share dividend. You would receive $0.15 per share in the quarters ended June 30 and September 30 and most likely $0.30 in the quarter ending on December 31. If you owned 100 shares, you would receive $0.60 multiplied by 100 shares, or $60 for the year.

You can find out the annual dividends a company pays by reading the stock pages of most major newspapers. Stocks are listed according to the exchange they trade on—New York or American—or on the over-the-counter (OTC) *National Association of Securities Dealers Automated Quotations system (NASDAQ)*. The newspapers list the companies in alphabetical order and typically show the company's ticker symbol (for the Coca-Cola Company, the ticker symbol is KO); the stock's closing price; change (up $0.50 or down $1.25, for example); volume traded in 100 shares; price-earnings ratio; dividends per share; *dividend yield* (annual dividend divided by current market price); and day's high and low prices.

We review cumulative, convertible, and callable preferred stock in Chapter 6.

National Association of Securities Dealers Automated Quotations system (NASDAQ) an exchangeless market because there is no physical exchange where stocks are traded. Brokers and dealers trade NASDAQ-listed securities directly with each other by phone or computer.

dividend yield the annual dividend payout in dollars divided by the current market value of the common stock ($1 annual dividend divided by $25 market price equals 4 percent dividend yield).

As was the case with income securities, you should consider dividend-paying securities as part of your asset class allocated toward the production of current income. With preferred stocks, the dividend is typically a fixed amount of money, similar to a bond that pays a fixed rate of interest or fixed coupon. Typically, the market price of a share of preferred stock fluctuates based on the credit rating (safety) of the issuer and the market yield for similar instruments. When market interest rates and yields rise, one expects the market price of a share of a fixed-rate preferred stock to fall such that the preferred stock yield matches the market yield for similar instruments. This is similar to the market value of a bond.

With common stocks, over time companies often increase the quarterly dividend as the company grows and becomes more successful. For example, according to the Coca-Cola Company 1997 annual report, the company paid $0.50 dividends per share in 1996 and $0.56 per share in 1997. The market price of Coca-Cola Company common stock has increased over time. To the extent you invest in common stocks that pay dividends and the company has a history of increasing its dividends over time, this can provide an increasing source of periodic income as well as a hedge against inflation.

If you don't need such current income for daily spending, consider reinvesting your dividends and the interest income you receive in additional securities. Generally, you can reinvest your dividends and interest in more securities of the same type.

With a common stock *dividend reinvestment plan (DRIP)*, you can use your dividends to purchase additional shares of common stock from the company. The company will not pay you a cash dividend; instead, it will apply your dividend income to purchase additional shares of the company's common stock. The same concept applies to mutual funds where you have the option of receiving dividend and capital gains distributions in cash or purchasing additional shares in the mutual fund. If you hold such shares in a regular account your dividends will be taxed as ordinary income even though you reinvest your distribution in new shares of the fund. If you participate in such reinvestment plans, it is important that you keep accurate records. Once you pay tax on the dividend and capital gains distributions, those amounts become part of your basis; you do not have to pay tax on those amounts twice.

> **dividend reinvestment plan (DRIP)**   a program where holders of shares of common stock can elect to reinvest their quarterly dividends in additional shares of the common stock, sometimes at a discount.

Dividends represent dollars paid to you by someone who has already been taxed on those dollars. When the XYZ Company recognized a profit in the year past, it most likely paid corporate income taxes on that income. A company typically has two choices with respect to after-tax earnings: it can distribute the earnings to shareholders in the form of dividends or it can reinvest them in the business. In the case of reinvesting, the earnings the company holds are called *retained earnings*. The company may reinvest the earnings in the business by buying back shares of its common stock or may invest money in acquiring other companies.

> **retained earnings**   after-tax accounting earnings held by the company for reinvestment. Typically companies pay a portion of their earnings to common stockholders in the form of dividends and retain the remainder.

When XYZ's *board of directors* declare a dividend be paid to the shareholders of record on a certain date (the *record date*), you receive those dividends as income and you must pay income taxes on that dividend income. This is double taxation.

You might consider this factor of double taxation as you allocate your portfolio toward income- and non-income-producing investments. In the case of fixed-income investments such as corporate bonds that are subject to income taxes, you might consider purchasing those investments in a *tax-deferred* account such as an individual retirement account (IRA) or 401(k) plan. You might consider purchasing stocks that pay little or no dividends in a regular account.

board of directors group of professionals who govern a corporation or other organization, typically comprised of leaders in industry and top executives of the company. Shareholders vote to approve the election of directors.

record date the date on which the investor in a common or preferred stock is entitled to receive the dividend declared by the board of directors. If the investor sells the common stock the day after the record date, the seller will still receive the dividend because they remain owners until the settlement date.

tax-deferred paying a tax that is due in a future tax year rather than the present one. Moneys working toward retirement in an IRA-type account, for example, grow tax-deferred and the taxes due are paid only when the dollars are withdrawn from the plan. A recently created type of retirement account, known as the Roth IRA allows the moneys to be put in after they have been taxed and then withdrawn tax-free when you retire.

Capital Appreciation

To distinguish between and among income, dividends, and *capital appreciation* (the increase in the value of an investment held) we should consider why we made a particular investment. Investors who seek capital appreciation are more concerned that the market value of the securities in their portfolio and the value of their overall portfolio increase over time.

capital appreciation   the increase in the value of an investment held and not yet sold.

Let's consider fixed-income securities such as bonds. Most income-oriented investors purchase fixed-income securities to receive income every six months. Fixed-income securities also carry the possibility of capital appreciation. If market conditions are favorable—for example, market interest rates decline while you own the bond—the market value of the security would increase. For the income investor, capital appreciation is secondary to the generation of current income. For the investor seeking capital appreciation, income would be a secondary benefit.

When investors purchase common stocks that pay relatively high dividends, they typically purchase the stock with the expectation that the company will continue paying dividends for the entire expected holding period or investment horizon. In all likelihood, most investors also hope the company will be more and more profitable over time and increase the quarterly dividend every year or two. Then, the investor will receive greater dividend income over time and hopefully the market value of the stock will increase as well.

These investments would be allocated to that percentage of your investment capital aimed at generating relatively conservative and stable income.

That portion of your portfolio invested for the purposes of realizing capital appreciation would only incidentally look to receive income or earn dividends. The primary goal or objective attached to those dollars is increased value of the investments.

To determine just what percentage would be allocated in your case into each investment category—income, dividends, or capital appreciation—see Chapter 4, "Asset Allocation Techniques."

If you are seeking capital appreciation, after allocating those dollars that will be placed at greater risk than the income/dividend-producing dollars, the first and most logical place to go would be into growth-oriented investments. Consider investing in a mutual fund or number of common stocks whose objective is: growth, growth and income, emerging growth, or aggressive growth. If all goes well, the value of the shares of these funds should increase over time and produce that capital appreciation sought from these dollars.

PSYCHIC INCOME (PRIDE, SLEEP WELL AT NIGHT FACTOR)

Many of us shy away from risk. Our risk tolerance level may be relatively low and we want to know that our portfolio will meet our financial needs. We like a degree of certainty. We may experience a certain pride of ownership of certain assets, irrespective of the return, and seek that peace of mind that enables us to sleep at night. Some people take a sentimental view toward investments; for example, one person we worked with received shares of common stock because his grandfather bequeathed the stock to him, and the person held on to the stock because it had sentimental value. This frequently applies to shares of a stock owned in a company we may have worked for all of our lives.

People must be comfortable with their portfolios and their investment decisions. Accordingly, they should consider allocating a certain percentage of their money—and this percentage will vary from person to person—into investments or classes of investments that satisfy these needs and wants.

Perhaps this would entail investing those dollars into shares of companies that are a part of the fabric of our country (automobiles, housing, aircraft, energy, manufacturing, etc.). Stocks or bonds of issues from this group may or may not grow dramatically in value or follow the broad market up during strong rallies, but will afford you that pride of ownership that can only result from holding such issues in your portfolio. As an owner of the bluest of the blue chips, as it were, you are saying to yourself that you have investments in things that would come apart only if the rest of the economy (global as well as domestic economy) were to come apart. Consumers will always use electric power, talk on the telephone, own an automobile, fly in a jet aircraft, or buy the daily groceries, and will want to/need to for the rest of their lives. These issues may never announce a new invention, discovery, innovation, or development that would otherwise drive the stock sky-high, but they are providing necessities to the world every day, day in and day out.

Stocks and/or bonds in this group needn't be confined to domestic issues only. The major countries of the world all are providing their citizenship with energy, communications, transportation, and food, and investors can participate in these companies either directly, through *American depositary receipts (ADRs)*—shares in foreign companies held in trust by the foreign branches of American banks (*American depositary shares (ADSs)*, or international and global mutual funds.

American depositary receipts (ADRs)   negotiable receipts traded in the United States that represent shares of a foreign company. These shares are held in trust by a trustee (typically a bank) for the benefit of the U.S. investor, who is entitled to receive all dividends and capital gains distributions from the foreign shares.

American depositary shares (ADSs)   typically used interchangeably with ADRs, but the company that issued the stock rather than the trustee holds the ADSs.

CAPITAL GAINS (REALIZED AND UNREALIZED)

Earlier in this chapter we discussed capital appreciation. Typically, capital appreciation is in the form of capital gains: an increase in the value of an investment. Suppose you purchase a share of Intel Corporation common stock at $75 per share and later the share is valued at $90 per share. Your capital gain would equal $15 ($90 minus $75). Investors have the choice of taking (realizing) capital gains or leaving them intact (unrealized capital gains) to hopefully grow. Always check with your own financial planner or adviser to decide whether to realize a capital gain and your personal tax adviser to determine the tax consequences resulting from realizing gains. When you invest in mutual funds, the mutual fund is required to distribute at least 95 percent of its income to the fund's shareholders every year, so when you own mutual fund shares, you are likely to realize a certain amount of capital gains through distributions every year regardless of whether you sell your mutual fund shares. Since there are several ways you can be taxed on mutual funds, we suggest that you obtain a copy of IRS Publication 564 on mutual fund distributions.

Realized Capital Gains

Simply put, a *realized capital gain* is a gain that has been taken—you sold an investment at a price higher than the price at which you acquired the investment. With mutual funds, realized capital gains result from transactions where the mutual fund portfolio manager sells securities in the mutual fund portfolio. Realizing a capital gain results in the creation of a *taxable event*. Suppose you acquired a share of Intel common stock for $75 per share and the market value of that stock appreciated to $90 since your purchase. Were you to sell the stock at its current value of $90 per share, the difference between your selling and buying prices, or $15, would be your realized capital gain: $90 selling price minus $75 purchase price equals $15 realized capital gain.

realized capital gain   a gain that has been taken—you sold an investment at a price higher than the price at which you acquired it.

taxable event   usually the sale of an asset at a gain or loss which would be used on that year's tax return; a realized gain or realized loss. The simple act of buying a security and holding on to it while it goes up in value represents a paper profit that isn't taxable since the gain was unrealized.

(For the sake of our example, we have omitted the cost to purchase and sell the securities—commissions. But you need to include the commissions to calculate your actual *gain* or *loss*. Always consult your own tax professional when realizing a gain from the sale of mutual funds in order to use the correct basis when calculating that gain. The IRS leaves the choice up to the taxpayer.)

gain   the amount of money by which the market value of a security exceeds the purchase price of that security. If you purchased a share of ABC Company common stock for $43 and today the market value of that stock is $52, your gain would equal $9.

The $15 gain you realized is taxed as a capital gain and not as ordinary income. In general, you can offset capital gains against capital losses.

This way you can reduce your net capital gains and your taxable income. As a result of the Taxpayer Relief Act of 1997, capital gains are subject to the following rates and long-term capital gains are taxed at lower rates than ordinary income:

Transaction Date	Holding Period	Maximum Tax Rate
On or after July 29, 1997	More than 18 months	20% (10% if otherwise qualify for 15% ordinary income tax rate)
On or after July 29, 1997	More than 1 year, but not more than 18 months	28%
On or after July 29, 1997	1 year or less	Ordinary income tax rates
On or after January 1, 2001	More than 5 years	20% (8% if otherwise qualify for 15% ordinary income tax rate)
On or after January 1, 2006	More than 5 years	18%

As you can see from the above example, if your capital appreciated and you sold the securities and realized the gains, when you pay the long-term, lower capital gains income taxes, you will be able to retain more of the money for reinvestment, spending, charitable donation, or whatever you prefer.

Tax considerations play an important role in investment decisions and strategies, and a lack of such knowledge can increase your risk. It is

loss the amount by which the market value of a security has declined below the price at which you purchased it. If you purchased one share of ABC Company common stock at $26 and the current market value equals $16, your loss equals $10.

always suggested that you consult a tax professional when dealing with investments. (Since tax legislation is constantly subject to change, modification, adjustment, and correction, please consult your tax professional on a regular basis to take advantage of and comply with the most current regulations.)

Unrealized Capital Gains

While realized capital gains are gains taken and taxed in the year you sell the securities, unrealized capital gains are simply gains made in securities and not taken. Unrealized capital gains remain tax-deferred until you sell the securities. Using the earlier example of a stock purchased at $75 per share and now worth $90 per share, we still have the same amount of gain ($15 per share owned), but the gain stays in your brokerage account as *paper profit*.

paper profit   the unrealized difference between the purchase price of any investment and its current higher value. For example, you bought a stock a number of years ago and invested $5000; today that same stock is worth $10,000; you have an unrealized profit of $5000. Paper profits aren't taxable until and unless realized.

Unrealized gains should be left alone, especially if the company whose stock you own is still growing and you expect future incremental appreciation, and you have no reason to sell the securities. Additionally, unrealized gains on securities still growing in tax-deferred retirement accounts can be left to grow until you retire. A third case can be made for unrealized gains in securities held in the accounts of children. Since the child will not need the moneys until college or another future event, the gains can be left to continue to grow tax-deferred until that time comes and enjoy the magic of compounding over time.

One potential risk with unrealized capital gains is that the market value of your securities may decline. That share of Intel common stock may decline in value from $90 to $75 or even less. Once you realize the gain, you pay the commissions and the capital gains tax. The net capital gain is your money to keep.

IS HOLDING ONE'S OWN A REWARD?

Owning an investment and watching it remain at or near the price you paid for the security really isn't a reward, but a loss. You pay an opportunity cost of money. In other words, you could have invested in a T-bill or *money market mutual fund* and earned a higher rate of return on that otherwise idle or nonworking capital.

> **money market mutual fund**   a mutual fund that invests in money market instruments.

What do you lose if you buy a stock at $45 per share and one year later it is still selling at $45 per share? Unless the entire marketplace has remained unchanged, interest rates and other economic factors are still where they were when you originally bought that stock, and no increases in dividends or interest have been announced, then you face the loss of investment opportunity and loss due to idle equity.

Perhaps during that period when your holdings merely marked time other categories of investments trended higher. You may have been holding one class of security while the growth group took off; your solid, old-line blue chips paid those regular dividends but didn't budge in price, while the high techs doubled in value—two simple examples of opportunity lost because of improper allocation of assets and poor market timing. That being said, the objective of asset allocation is to split your money across different asset classes precisely so that one asset class increases in value while another class stays the same or declines in value. The key is to set up your overall portfolio to succeed.

Idle equity, on the other hand, could be in the form of the equity in assets held and not used for other investments. You own a home that is worth $300,000 but has only a $100,000 mortgage. You have $200,000 in equity in your home: $300,000 market value minus $100,000 mortgage. Your house contains idle or untapped equity in the amount of $200,000. If you can borrow 80 percent of the fair market value, or $240,000 (80 percent of $300,000), and your outstanding mortgage balance equals $100,000, then you can borrow an additional $140,000.

You can use the idle $140,000 as the down payment on a three-family house (rental property) for, say, $350,000, with a $210,000 mortgage of its own, which is producing income sufficient to service the mortgage, pay the expenses, and throw off annual income or free cash flow. Now you still own that $300,000 principal residence and that $350,000 income property as well. All you have to do is arrange the numbers to work for you. That being said, you may not want to tap the equity value in your home. We have worked with people who have borrowed money against the equity value in their homes, made poor investments, and subsequently lost their investments and their homes.

A similar case can be made using that portfolio of income-producing blue-chip stocks or bonds that is worth $250,000, paying you $12,500 per year in dividends or interest income. If that account were to be margined (taking out a portion of the equity using the value of the portfolio as collateral) and you borrowed $100,000 "from yourself," you could reinvest that margined money back into additional stocks or bonds or even into a piece of income-producing property or other worthwhile investment suitable to your investment objectives and goals. Here, again, you still own the initial portfolio, which is still producing that $12,500 per year in income, and whatever other suitable investments were made with the margined dollars. The key is to generate a positive rate of return on the margin debt.

A tax benefit is gained from a margined transaction since the margin interest is treated as an investment expense and the dividends or interest income on the portfolio are investment income. With certain limitations, you can offset the margin interest expense against the investment income. Consider putting that idle equity to work, prudently, and capture the opportunity value of those dollars.

IS REWARD NECESSARILY MEASURED IN DOLLARS?

As we have already pointed out, the peace of mind factor can and should be considered a reward. The ability to sleep at night while your portfolio may only stand still is another reward. The knowledge that your investments are doing what you need to get done and will be available for you when you need them and remain reasonably intact is definitely a reward. The growth in the value of a portfolio in the form of unrealized profits (paper profits), is a reward. The fact that your risk tolerance level is being addressed with your current portfolio and its allocation is a reward. Reward does not have to be in the form of dollars.

WHAT TO DO IF AN INVESTMENT DOES NOT REWARD YOU

This may sound like an oversimplification, but the fact of the matter is, as it applies especially to the world of investing, if an investment is not doing what you bought it to do over a prolonged period of time or has stopped doing what you bought it to do, or market conditions have changed, you should sell it. Channel your dollars to other more productive investments. You may decide that your investments are underperforming when the rate of return is less than the benchmark or performs in the bottom quartile (25 percent) of investments in its class for two to three years in a row.

Before you switch your investments or change your asset allocation, compare your underperforming or nonperforming investments against other investments in the same asset class. That particular asset class may be in slump. And that is precisely the goal of asset allocation. If an entire asset class is having a down period, hold the asset if it still meets your criteria and fits your asset allocation. Don't change your portfolio composition without careful thought, analysis, and planning, because, just at the moment you move those dollars out of the underperforming asset category, those securities may be poised for a takeoff.

Asset Allocation Techniques

CREATING ASSET ALLOCATION

Once you determine your needs and objectives, you can begin to shape your portfolio. That entails allocating your assets to the particular asset classes that will enable you to achieve your financial goals. This means creating asset allocation.

Earlier in this book, we used a pizza pie as an analogy for asset allocation. Recall the last time you went to pick up that pizza you ordered. While you waited for your order, you probably watched the cook throw a little flour on the marble slab, take a ball of dough from the refrigerator, stretch that dough into the shape of the pie, add tomato sauce, sprinkle on some cheese and maybe even add a few other toppings before sliding the pie into the oven. In one sense, that is how you begin to create an asset allocation. You make your own pizza, slicing your portfolio or asset pie into pieces that match your needs, your goals, your time horizons, and other criteria.

POPULAR ASSET ALLOCATION METHODS

The financial community has developed a number of asset allocation methods. These models include: the "100 minus your age" model, the financial objectives model, the cash flow needs model, the risk tolerance model, tactical asset allocation, and the brokerage house model, as well as 100 percent common stocks for the long run. Each of these models has its merits and flaws and we will discuss each one in the following paragraphs.

"100 Minus Your Age" Model

Under this model, you decide which percentage of your investment portfolio to invest in common stocks based on the formula "100 minus your age." This model assumes you will live to be approximately 100 years old and can afford to assume less and less risk as you get older.

As you can see from Table 4.1, you simply subtract your age from 100 and allocate your assets accordingly. A 30-year-old person would use 70 percent–30 percent, where you would invest 70 percent of your portfolio in equities and 30 percent in fixed income. As the person gets older, he or she would reduce the percentage of money allocated to equities.

The drawback with this model is that it does not take into account a person's life expectancy, wealth, and financial needs, or inflation. If history repeats itself, life expectancy will increase, the cost of living will rise, and common stocks will continue to be an effective hedge against inflation. Under this model, every year the investor reduces the percentage of the portfolio that is invested in equities. As a result, over time the portfolio is likely to generate more current income and less growth. This may be detrimental to one's financial health over the long run, especially considering inflation and increased life expectancies.

Financial Objectives Model

This asset allocation model encompasses determining your financial objectives and their respective time horizons and allocating your money ac-

TABLE 4.1 Asset Allocation: "100 Minus Your Age"			
Your Age	"100 Minus Your Age"	Percentage to Equities	Percentage to Fixed Income
30	70	70%	30%
40	60	60	40
50	50	50	50
60	40	40	60
70	30	30	70

cordingly. Perhaps you want to take a vacation next summer. This is a specific goal that has a relatively short time horizon, perhaps 12 months. Determine the cost of your vacation and make a spending budget for your vacation. Then save money equal to the cost of your trip. Since you expect this event (goal) to occur in a very short period of time, you will need your money to pay the vacation costs and cannot afford to assume significant market risk. Save your money in a high-quality money market mutual fund, U.S. Treasury bill, savings account, or certificate of deposit. Your goal should be to preserve your principal, earn interest income, and not reap great returns. In terms of asset allocation, you should allocate this money toward low-risk or risk-free investments (see Chapter 5).

You can make similar decisions regarding your other objectives, including buying a car or home, funding a wedding or college tuition, and funding retirement. Depending on your investment (time) horizon and your tolerance for risk, you will allocate your money to more or less risky investments.

Cash Flow Needs Model

This asset allocation model encompasses assessing your cash flow needs (spending budget) and cash flow sources (income sources). The first step in this model is to establish a spending budget. In other words, how much money do you need for living expenses? Once you determine how much money you will need for spending, you can calculate your total sources of income. Sources of income and cash flow typically include:

- ✔ Wages, salary.
- ✔ Pension payments (defined benefit plans).
- ✔ Social Security payments.
- ✔ Retirement plan distributions (defined contribution).
- ✔ Tax-deferred annuity withdrawals.
- ✔ Interest income.
- ✔ Dividend income.
- ✔ Capital gains.
- ✔ Principal (investments).
- ✔ Inheritances (we recommend that you don't rely on this source of income until you actually receive the money).
- ✔ Income from sale of residence.
- ✔ Income from sale of stuff (cars, boats, vacation homes, etc.).

The key is to match up your spending (income) needs and your sources of income. Then determine whether you have enough assets (large enough investment portfolio) to attain your goals. If you are confident that you have enough assets so you can attain your goals, then it is possible that you can select a relatively conservative asset allocation. Such an asset allocation would emphasize current income rather than capital appreciation. Of course, this strategy does not leave room for error, rising costs, and a greater life expectancy.

Project the asset shortfall. This is the amount of money that you need to accumulate in order to achieve your financial goals. You can accumulate this amount of money by decreasing your spending, channeling more of your money to your investment portfolio, and tilting a higher percentage of your portfolio toward growth assets with the objective of earning higher returns.

If you project that your assets (investments) and sources of income will fall short of your income needs, then it is likely that you will have to adopt a more aggressive asset allocation that emphasizes capital appreciation and growth. To achieve such rates of return, it is likely that you will have to invest more of your portfolio in growth assets such as common stocks.

Once you project an asset shortfall, then you can determine how much money you need to invest now and the rate of return you need to achieve to attain your financial goals. If you calculate the market value of your portfolio today and the amount of money you need to accumulate by a target date (for example, your retirement date), you can calculate a target rate of return.

Assume you need to earn a 7 percent rate of return on your portfolio in order to achieve your financial goals. Suppose the rate of return on high-grade corporate bonds is approximately 5.5 percent and the long-term rate of return on the S&P 500 (common stocks) is approximately 10.5 percent. If these rates of return continue in the future and you invest half of your money in each category, your average rate of return should equal 8 percent. You can blend expected rates of return in this fashion and calculate an approximate target rate of return. However, past returns will not necessarily continue and repeat themselves in the future.

If you have a large shortfall and a relatively short investment time horizon, you should reduce your spending and consider investing in assets that have the potential to yield greater rates of return.

If you have a relatively long investment time horizon and need a relatively small amount of money to bridge your gap, then you can channel a larger percentage of your portfolio toward more conservative income-producing investments.

Risk Tolerance Model

This asset allocation model ignores financial calculations and emphasizes psychology. In other words, a risk-averse person would invest most or all of his or her investment portfolio in conservative investments. The theory is that the individual will sleep more comfortably knowing that the portfolio is relatively safe and secure. These would include the low-risk investments described in Chapter 5. Of course, this model ignores inflation and life expectancy.

Tactical Asset Allocation

This asset allocation model is effectively an asset timing effort. Under this asset allocation method, the portfolio consists of a combination of common stocks, bonds, and cash. The investment manager switches the allocations among the three asset classes in an effort to maximize the portfolio returns. The goal is to load up on common stocks at the bottom of the bear market, just before common stocks are poised to soar in value. Researchers have conducted many studies on this methodology, and they have all concluded that market timing rarely, if ever, works.

Brokerage House Model

This asset allocation model combines the cash flow needs model and the risk tolerance model. The brokerage house recommends a suggested portfolio among common stocks, bonds, cash, and commodities. We follow this model, with emphasis on cash flow needs.

100 Percent Common Stocks for the Long Run

This method means allocating your long-term money, especially funds for retirement, 100 percent to common stocks. This strategy has become increasingly popular, especially as the bull market has roared since 1982. Over time, stocks as well as other asset classes experience bear markets. So, it may or may not be wise to allocate all of your money to common stocks.

MODELING AN ASSET ALLOCATION

Creating asset allocation begins with self-examination. Some of the questions you need to consider when putting together an asset allocation model start with a visit to your personal physician. We're not suggesting that anyone try to play God, but that physician knows you and your medical history and can estimate your life expectancy. Knowing your life expectancy and family history can help you determine how long, all things being equal, you will need your money and how much money you will need. This can help you manage your assets over your lifetime and prepare for any illnesses you can reasonably expect to contract.

Now you have a time line to work from that will enable you to project how many years there are between now and when that last child is finished with college/grad school; how many weddings you have to pay for and approximately when they will take place; how much longer you will need that family residence before you and your spouse can move into that beachfront or golf course condominium and abandon all the space a growing family requires.

Estimating your approximate life expectancy will enable you to schedule that retirement date; the date you begin to collect Social Security and pension income and when you begin drawing from your retirement plans and annuities; when it makes sense to access your tax-deferred accounts; and when to begin to spend the principal and give away the excess. What sort of a lifestyle do you want to enjoy during those 20 or 30 or more years you will be retired? You know, as we enter the next century, it is likely that retired people will be in retirement as long as or longer than they worked. Will we travel a lot, play a lot, spend a lot, spend a little?

You must address all of these issues in order to create a financial plan and suitable asset allocation for yourself. Be sure to factor in a number that is reasonable (for example, 5 percent to 7 percent) to account for future inflation (loss of buying power over the years). The long-run inflation rate has been approximately 3 percent and as we go to press with this book, economists forecast little or no inflation. But that seems unrealistic, especially over the long run. If you assume a 5 percent to 7 percent rate of inflation and manage your money accordingly and your returns exceed your plan, you will have more wealth than you anticipated.

INCOME SOURCES

Everyone will want to stop working at some point, and in order to do so, one slice of your pie, marked "retirement," must be carved out and evaluated by looking at the following sources of income:

✔ *Social Security.* Ask the Social Security Administration to send you a printout of your current account. Contact the Social Security Administration by calling 1-800-772-1213 and request Form SSA-7004. Make sure all of your annual contributions have been recorded accurately. Find out how much in benefits you and your spouse would receive at your normal retirement ages. Since Social Security is *indexed* to inflation and has increased with the cost of living, your benefits should keep pace with inflation. You now have one source of income in retirement. Unfortunately, Social Security may be reduced or eliminated in the future. Be sure to plan accordingly.

> **indexed**   the tying of taxes, wages, and so on to one or more of the broad indexes followed by economists so they would rise or fall with the index.

✔ *Defined Benefit Pensions.* these pension plans represent a fixed amount of money you will receive every month, beginning when you retire and ending when you or your spouse dies (depending on how you set up your distributions). Unions and some corporations offer defined benefit pensions. This may represent another source of retirement income.

In many ways, Social Security payments and defined benefit pension payments represent fixed-income streams. Your receipt of these benefits or payment streams depends on the financial strength or creditworthiness of the Social Security Administration and the party paying the defined benefits.

✔ *Tax-Deferred Investments.* These include 403(b) plan assets, 401(k) plan assets, individual retirement accounts (IRAs), and other tax-deferred accounts. What is the current value of the portfolio? How much money will you add to these plans between now and when you retire? What is a reasonable growth rate for your investments (use a conservative 5 percent to 7 percent per year) between now and retirement? You now have another source of potential retirement income.

✔ *Current Investments/Savings.* How much have you accumulated in your nonretirement portfolio and savings accounts? How much will you add to these accounts between now and retirement? How much do you expect these assets to appreciate (grow) between now and your retirement? This fourth amount added to the three above will give you the money available at retirement to live on.

If the above calculations produce enough income for your purposes, that is the size of the portion of your portfolio allocated toward retirement, and it doesn't have to be increased. If not, some pro rata amount must be added to make up the difference. But, you know the size of your retirement needs and objectives and how much your portfolio needs to grow or if your portfolio can be left to grow on its own.

AT-RISK ASSETS

In Chapter 2, we discussed risk tolerance and how to assess whether you have a high or low risk tolerance. The amount of your assets you are prepared to lose can go into this slice of the pie. As a general rule of thumb, the younger you are and the more years you have to replace assets lost, the greater the percentage of your portfolio you can place at risk. The older you are and the less likely you will be able to replace losses, the less money you should have at risk. Earlier in this chapter we discussed the cash flow needs model. We considered growth assets, more aggressive rates of return, and the amount of risk one needs to assume to achieve a target rate of return. Consider these factors in light of your financial position.

- ✔ *Children's Weddings.* How many children do you have that need to be married off by you? How old are they now? When are they likely to get married? What kind of wedding are they expecting? What kind of a wedding did you promise them? How much will that wedding cost?

- ✔ *Children's Education.* How many children do you have who are likely to enroll in college? How many of them should consider technical training instead of that Ivy League college? How much do colleges charge now and how much more will they likely be charging when your children enroll? (Add an inflation factor of 8 percent to 10 percent per year here to be conservative.) What level and kind of education do your children need to excel in their chosen fields? What level of higher education did you promise them? How much will that tuition and those expenses cost? How much of that tuition do you want to fund? Can your children borrow money to fund their tuition?

If you see those amounts in and among your current assets, allocate those dollars into this group. If not, project how much money you have to add to this growing group to reach the mark you have established.

✔ *Income-Producing Assets.* These are those dollars that you have put into bonds, CDs, money market accounts, savings, and so on, that don't necessarily grow in principal, but produce monthly, quarterly, or semiannual income that is either to be spent or reinvested. As you age and have a lower risk tolerance, this segment should make up a larger and larger percentage of your portfolio. In your formative years, say under 55, this should probably be among the smallest categories of your asset allocation model.

The amount of risk you are prepared to accept at various ages, using differing assets, is discussed in much more detail in Chapters 5, 6, and 7.

As you can see, in just a few pages we have identified several separate asset allocation categories or areas into which you could allocate those dollars. A little introspection will help uncover additional areas that fit your individual and personal requirements.

Perhaps you like to gamble. Allocate a percentage of those dollars toward visits to Atlantic City or Las Vegas, during which you will be ready to lose every penny without blinking an eye. Perhaps you favor large gifts to charities, hospitals, and churches, and feel good doing so; allocate enough dollars to satisfy that personal need/desire. Perhaps you like to drive a very expensive car and replace it every year regardless of the financial considerations; put $50,000 or so into that category and go for it. In other words, whatever you need, you want, you wish to do, or you have to accomplish will determine the number of slices necessary and the amounts of money put into each slice of our portfolio or asset allocation.

ALLOCATING FOR GOALS
VERSUS ACROSS ALL YOUR ASSETS

As mentioned, there are things you want/like to do, need to accomplish, feel good about contributing to that transcend allocating assets for the sake of pure investment or financial considerations. Your personal goal may be to fund your children's or grandchildren's college education or weddings. Just put aside enough dollars to make it happen. Schedule a monthly contribution from your current earnings that will make those personal goals possible over your desired time frame. But make sure that you provide for yourself and your spouse first. Most likely your children will be able to afford to incur and service debt, whereas you will have less capacity to pay off debt once you retire. As with so much of asset allocation, the key word is *you*.

There is no reason to have to justify to anyone or explain to anyone those whims and goals you have set for yourself. Whatever it is that you want or need to do should be the goal for however many dollars it takes to do it. Just plan accordingly.

SLICING UP THE PIE TO FIT *YOU*

By now it should be clear that no two people's asset allocation models will be exactly the same. Even if two people are the same age, are in about the same income bracket, own the same amount of assets, live in similar houses, drive similar cars, and so forth, each person has his or her own unique personality, interests, and goals. This can apply to the assets of a husband and wife. Just because two people are married to one another doesn't mean that their respective assets have to be invested or allocated in the same manner. One spouse may be interested in collectibles while the other may be happy only with U.S. government bonds. The husband may only live for the moment while the wife looks at tomorrow and tomorrow. A remarried couple may have separate sets of children with separate goals and wishes for them; one may want to play golf every day while the other wants to play the stock market every day. You can see that *you* crops up again and again when you have to slice up that pie.

Perhaps the best way to illustrate how to slice up the pie would be to do just that—slice one up.

HOW MANY EGGS SHOULD BE IN THE BASKET?

As facetious as this sounds, the answer is as many eggs as it takes for you to realize your financial plan and attain your financial goals. Each person's investment portfolio and asset allocation should be tailored to the individual's personality, style, and needs.

If you want to live on the same amount of income in retirement as you were earning while working and make no adjustments to your way of living, lifestyle, spending habits, and the like, you will have to see to it that your retirement slice has enough assets allocated to it and added to it on a regular basis to reach that figure. Be sure to account for inflation as well. If you are more realistic and expect to live on 70 percent or 80 percent of your preretirement income, as most retirees do and are expected to continue to do, then the retirement account needs enough "eggs" to produce income at that rate.

Earlier we spoke of children's education, weddings, trips, and automobiles. You can calculate just how much those events and purchases will cost. That's how many eggs you need in that particular category—enough to make it happen and happen on your timetable. As you can see, there is no magic to all this, just a hard look at yourself and a realistic evaluation of your needs, your objectives, your goals and wants, and your personal financial life cycles.

SAMPLE ASSET ALLOCATION

In this example, let's assume our investor is 40 years old and intends to retire at age 65. Here is how he or she might analyze current financial position, potential sources of retirement income, and asset and investment needs. The following example contains financial calculations and makes certain assumptions about rates of returns and life expectancy. As with all monetary examples and financial projections, it is important to consult your own financial advisers; the information contained in this sample asset allocation may not be applicable to you.

The following points highlight the assumptions we are making about the investor's financial position:

- ✔ Current age: 40 years old.
- ✔ Intended retirement age: 65 (would like to stop working for wages completely at that time).
- ✔ Current annual salary income: $45,000.
- ✔ Expects to receive $75,000 in defined pension benefits every year after reaching age 65. This represents 50 percent of projected final year of salary income.
- ✔ Expects to receive $24,000 in Social Security benefits every year once he or she reaches age 65.

✔ Inflation rate will equal 3 percent per year. However, to be conservative we will assume that inflation will equal 5 percent per year (this tactic leaves room for error in the event inflation exceeds our expectations, investment returns are less than anticipated, or income needs and spending exceed our plan).

✔ Investor will spend 100 percent of the income in retirement that he or she earns in the last year worked (at age 64). Many people spend approximately 70 percent to 80 percent of their preretirement income during retirement and this may be a reasonable assumption for you. If you intend to spend less money during retirement (and this is difficult to predict), then it may be reasonable to save less money for retirement.

✔ Has retirement plan portfolio assets with a current value of $55,000.

✔ Estimates life expectancy to be 85 years. Therefore, he can reasonably expect to live for another 20 years after retirement at age 65. An investor who outlives life expectancy is likely to run out of money. Second, if cost of living exceeds plan, then investor is likely to drain investment portfolio at too fast a rate. In other words, spending too much money early on would cause earning assets to be depleted and portfolio's earning power to be reduced as well.

Someone who currently earns $45,000 will need to earn approximately $152,500 in 25 years with the impact of inflation just to maintain the same purchasing power. We calculated this amount by compounding $45,000 at 5 percent per year for 25 years. If you assume a 3 percent rate of inflation, then one would need to earn approximately $94,500.

If $152,500 in annual income is needed during retirement years and someone expects to receive $75,000 in pension benefits and $24,000 in Social Security benefits, the retiree needs to generate $53,500 in incremental spendable dollars every year during retirement. We calculated this amount as follows: $152,500 minus $75,000 minus $24,000 equals $53,500. Therefore, this person's retirement plan and other investments have to generate $53,500 per year during his retirement. It is important to estimate the income tax consequences. Use pretax or after-tax income.

The retiree will need to generate this amount of money for 20 years, which is his or her assumed retirement lifetime. Under these assumptions, he or she can spend the income that the portfolio generates and spend a portion of the principal. This strategy assumes exhausting one's wealth by 85 years of age and not leaving any money to heirs.

A few more assumptions:

✔ Once our friend retires, he or she will continue to invest money and will achieve a 6 percent overall rate of return. But, if we consider the inflation rate to be 3 percent, then while he or she may earn 6 percent on the money, 3 percent of the money will be lost to inflation. Therefore, the net pretax, postinflation rate of return is 3 percent.

✔ If the person intends to spend $53,500 per year for 20 years and expects to earn a 3 percent rate of return on the portfolio, at retirement he or she will need a portfolio that has a then current value (future value) of approximately $795,950.

✔ If he or she follows the same assumptions as above but expects the portfolio to generate a rate of return equal to 5 percent per annum, at retirement the portfolio should have a value of approximately $666,750.

As mentioned earlier, suppose the current value of the investment portfolio equals $55,000 and those assets need to grow to $795,950 in 25 years. If the investor prefers not to add any more money to the investment portfolio, he or she will have to earn a compound annual rate of return of 11.28 percent. Considering that the long-term rate of return on the S&P 500 Index of common stocks has equaled approximately 10.5 percent, this target rate of return may be somewhat unrealistic.

Suppose that our friend rethinks the financial plan and decides to invest more money every year for the next 25 years. Investing $1000 every year would mean needing to achieve a rate of return equal to only 10.63 percent per year. Electing to invest $2000 per year would mean needing to achieve a rate of return equal to 10.02 percent.

Let's take our example one step further. Suppose our friend can invest money through a qualified retirement program and can take an income tax deduction equal to the contribution in the year of the contribution. Someone who pays income taxes at the rate of 30 percent saves $0.30 in income taxes for every dollar contributed to these plans (subject to limits). Therefore, if he or she makes a pretax contribution of $2000 and saves 30 percent or $600 due to the income tax deduction, he or she contributes only $1400 in after-tax dollars into the fund.

Let's consider one more factor in our example. Suppose the employer matches retirement plan contributions dollar-for-dollar (100 percent) up to $2000. Now, our friend invests $1400 in after-tax money and actually increases his or her retirement plan assets by $4000 in pretax dollars. Now an annual rate of return of only 8.89 percent is needed. This is powerful. Be sure to analyze all the rules and limits regarding the retirement plans available to you.

SHOULD ALL YOUR EGGS BE IN ONE BASKET?

In some very rare cases, yes, but in general, no. For the informed, sophisticated, professional investor, perhaps yes. There are numerous stories of the early employees of America's great growth companies who have become millionaires because they invested in a company's common stock early in the company's growth cycle. Examples include McDonald's, Wal-Mart, Dell Computer, Home Depot, Microsoft, and Intel, to name a few. For most of us, it pays to diversify and allocate our money across many different asset classes.

Consider your junket to the casino. To place your entire bet on one of the 36 numbers on the roulette table is senseless. There are 35 other possibilities, not counting the zero and double-zero, and the odds of your losing are high. The same logic applies to making investments, since you are betting on the management of one company, the powers that be of one government, or one company's products and its ability to sell them. Review Chapter 1 and reread the section "Allocation versus Diversification"; then consider the above.

If you were a billionaire and purchased only tax-exempt bonds, planning to hold them all to maturity and just live on the millions of dollars of annual income, it probably wouldn't matter that all your eggs were in the fixed-income, tax-exempt, muni arena. But since most of us aren't billionaires, we must diversify our investments to spread our risk among as many categories as our assets will allow and invest for growth.

Let's continue our example.

If our friend's goal is to realize an annual rate of return of 8.89 percent and we assume that the rate of return on cash and other relatively low-risk assets equals 4 percent, the rate of return on medium-risk assets equals 6 percent, and the rate of return on relatively high-risk investments equals 10 percent, then the portfolio could be allocated as follows:

Cash and other low-risk assets:	5 percent
Medium-risk assets:	20 percent
High-risk assets:	75 percent

Alternatively, the portfolio could be allocated as follows:

Cash and other low-risk assets:	0 percent
Medium-risk assets:	25 percent
High-risk assets:	75 percent

There are numerous other allocations that may achieve the same target rate of return.

Suppose the investor reviews his allocation and decides that allocating 75 percent to common stocks and other relatively high-risk assets is too much. He or she may be more comfortable allocating 50 percent to medium-risk assets and 50 percent to high-risk assets. If we assume that the historical rates of return for these asset classes will repeat themselves, then the expected rate of return would equal 8 percent per annum.

The investor's goal is to grow assets that have a current value of $55,000 into $795,950 over 25 years. In our earlier examples, we assumed that he or she needed to achieve a certain rate of return and then would allocate assets accordingly. In this scenario, the investor expects to achieve an 8 percent rate of return per annum. Following these assumptions, to achieve desired goals, approximately $5740 needs to be contributed to the portfolio every year. When this amount is contributed to a qualified retirement plan as described below, after-tax contributions for someone who pays income taxes at a 30 percent rate would equal $4018. This amount may be reduced by the amount of the employer's matching contribution.

Another way to analyze the asset allocation is to consider all sources of income and all portfolio assets. Our friend is eligible to receive Social Security benefits and defined pension benefits. In effect, one can consider these investments to be fixed-income-type investments. As before, assume that the annual income goal is $152,500, and the Social Security benefits equal $24,000 and the pension benefits equal $75,000. One can calculate the present value of these annuity streams. Using a 4 percent discount rate and assuming a 20-year payment horizon, the present value would equal approximately $1,345,450. Let's add this number to the value of the investor's other assets in 25 years, which equals $795,950: $2,141,400. Then, the percentage of money invested in relatively risky assets becomes less than 75 percent.

These examples assume that historical rates of return will occur in the future. This may or may not be the case. It is somewhat of an oversimplification that one can use a simple average to compute returns, but this is a relatively accurate method of analysis. In addition, in our experience, investors tend to be overly optimistic about their return projections. To protect yourself, you might assume that your investment returns will be less than you expect and you might want to save and invest additional funds.

Read Chapters 5, 6, and 7 to select suitable investments for you. Visit your local public library or search the Internet to research the various categories in the Moody's Investors Service books and the Standard & Poor's 500 Stock Index. Each of these reference sources breaks down global industry by the categories suggested (for example, growth, emerging growth, etc.). Review the Lipper Analytical Service along with the various mutual fund directories and analyses produced by a host of mutual fund associations to help you locate funds with the investment objectives listed from among the over 8000 different mutual funds in existence today.

Chapter

5

Low-Risk Assets

LOW-RISK ASSET CATEGORY EXPLAINED

Low-risk assets are assets that are relatively stable; you are likely to recover your investment, and the rate of return is relatively predictable.

Every one of us, the authors included, has a certain number of dollars or a certain percentage of our respective assets that are important to us for personal or financial security reasons. We wouldn't be willing to part with these assets or see the value of these assets dramatically diminished due to poor investment decisions, adverse market conditions, or even changes in the economy in general. These assets might also be considered no-risk assets as well. Of course, nothing is completely without risk, so when we speak of no-risk assets, we mean those assets that, all other things being equal, would remain intact while other assets would erode in value or even become valueless.

In this section, we will touch on a number of types of investments that are likely to continue to pay dividends and interest on a regular basis and at least maintain their face value at maturity or at the end of your target investment horizon. During changing market conditions, low-risk assets might drop in market value, but it is likely that they would decline in value less than other, more volatile asset classes.

We own a 5.75 percent, $10,000 face value U.S. Treasury bond that will mature in five years and pays us $575 per year in interest income. We receive a check for $237.50 every six months (one-half of $575). While the market value of this bond may decline during the bond's life, we are almost certain to receive our $10,000 at maturity.

We have learned that when interest rates rise, bond prices fall. In other words, there is an opposite or inverse relationship between interest rates and bond market prices. During this 5-year period, the market value of our $10,000 bond might be $9,550 at one point in time, $10,375 at another point, and even $8,750 at yet another point. But, we intend to hold this bond to maturity and continue to collect that $575 coupon every year for the next five years. Therefore, it doesn't matter where market conditions take the value of the bond during the bond's life. We care only that we are guaranteed that $10,000 in five years and that guarantee is backed by the U.S. government's ability to print money (full faith and credit, a guarantee that cannot be offered by anyone else).

The U.S. Treasury bond is just one example of the low-risk assets we will discuss in this chapter.

NATURE OF RISK

When we use the term "risk" we all have our own definition of what it means to us and just how much of our investments we are prepared to place at risk or lose.

A quick review of Chapter 2 will reveal at least a dozen types of risk and from it you will further learn that the word *you* is paramount when discussing risk and even more important when you divide up your assets according to your own risk tolerance level as it applies to a specific group of assets. No individual will have the identical level of risk tolerance of another and no two individuals would ever have the same asset allocation model (the division of assets according to your own understanding of your own ability to accept risk) except by pure chance or by following a financial adviser's asset allocation model verbatim without tailoring it to your specific circumstances. This applies to any two of you reading these pages and may apply to you and your spouse. Therefore, we will break down the various asset categories discussed into three broad groups:

✔ Low-risk assets—Chapter 5
✔ Medium-risk assets—Chapter 6.
✔ High-risk assets—Chapter 7.

The key is to find those investments that best meet your goals and objectives while understanding that each component of your portfolio involves assuming a different degree of risk with the dollars invested.

RISKS WITH LOW-RISK ASSETS

The major risk with the low-risk asset class is the absence of growth. The majority of these investments are relatively stable and they typically pay interest income. For most of the bonds, the interest coupons are fixed-dollar amounts throughout the entire life of the bond, payable semiannually. This means that the investor receives the same coupon every period. And inflation continues to eat away our purchasing power. Even with money market instruments where the rates fluctuate with market rates, the interest rates may be 4 percent to 5 percent per annum. After inflation and income taxes, this leaves little money left over for growth.

Another risk inherent in this asset class is the credit quality of the issuer. Treasury securities are backed by the full faith and credit of the U.S. Government. The marketplace assumes that these securities are riskless. The investor will recover his or her investment. Investors can manage their risk by selecting investments of the highest credit quality.

PLACE IN PORTFOLIO/PURPOSE

Remembering the asset allocation models discussed in Chapter 4 and keeping in mind that it may be acceptable for all your assets to be at little or no risk, our 40-year-old investor may have 25 percent to 45 percent of his or her assets in low or *no-risk investments* of the type to be described in this chapter. The purpose of this allocation is to allow the other 55 percent of your portfolio to grow and gain value through both appreciation and reinvestment. At the same time, the income-producing portion of the portfolio collects interest and dividends. These investments are designed to provide relatively stable income regardless of whether the market goes up, down, or sideways. This low- or no-risk segment also allows for that "peace of mind" or "sleep well at night" factor discussed in Chapter 3.

Here is a list of some of the reasons people invest in low-risk assets:

✔ For funds to meet a specific goal or purpose.
✔ For emergency spending money.
✔ For peace of mind.
✔ To reduce portfolio's volatility.

✔ To round out asset allocation.

✔ As temporary home for idle cash.

✔ As savings account for extra spending money.

✔ For tax-advantaged interest income (some issues with taxation).

no-risk investments   since we are all going to suffer from buying power risk over time, the only type of investment that can be said to be riskless would be one that isn't marketable and isn't subject to market risk. United States savings bonds, passbook savings accounts (up to the insured limits of the bank), and bank certificates of deposit (again, up to the insured limits of the bank) are nonmarketable, and therefore riskless, investments you could make.

Fixed-income securities comprise the largest segment of the universe of investments from a dollar standpoint. If you consider just *governments,* which include Treasury bills, Treasury notes, and Treasury bonds, as well as the whole world of federal *agency securities*, you are looking at many trillions of dollars in face value. That number probably exceeds the total value of all other securities combined.

governments   U.S. government obligations, including Treasury bills, Treasury notes, Treasury bonds, and the debt of various U.S. government agencies (agency securities).

agency securities   securities issued by an agency of the federal government such as the Federal National Mortgage Association or the Government National Mortgage Association. Such securities may or may not be direct obligations of the federal government, since it is the agency of the government rather than the government (the people) borrowing the money.

GOVERNMENT SECURITIES

For the purposes of this low-risk category, we will look at issues of the United States government and its agencies. Similar securities issued by the governments or government agencies of other countries should certainly be considered after due study is given to the track record, currency fluctuation, stability or lack thereof of the government, and other risk factors relating to the countries being considered. With foreign bonds, the portfolio manager may want to hedge the foreign exchange risk in the futures arena to protect your U.S. dollars.

United States Treasury Bonds

U.S. Treasury bonds (T-bonds) are securities that are essentially a loan to the U.S. federal government, backed by the full faith and credit of the U.S. Treasury. This guarantee translates into the ability of the U.S. Treasury to print money—a guarantee not available in the private sector. Treasury bonds are available in the secondary market that could mature next week, next year or as long as 30 years into the future. The Treasury issues these securities through Treasury Direct via auction. T-bonds pay interest on a semiannual basis. Such interest is subject to U.S. federal income taxes, but is exempt from state and local income taxes. Newly issued bonds mature in 10 to 30 years. These bonds trade in the secondary market in 32nds of a dollar. A typical price may be $99^{16}/_{32}$ or 99.5 percent of $10,000, which equals $9,950. If held to maturity, there would be no-risk involved since the U.S. Treasury agrees to pay the face amount of the bond when redeemed by you, the bondholder.

> **U.S. Treasury bonds (T-bonds)**   securities that are essentially a loan to the U.S. federal government, backed by the full faith and credit of the U.S. Treasury. Newly issued T-bonds mature in 10 to 30 years.

United States Treasury Notes

U.S. Treasury notes (T-notes) carry the same features as Treasury bonds: the guarantee, semi-annual interest, same income tax treatment of interest income, and availability in the secondary market or through Treasury Direct. There are two differences: T-notes are typically issued to mature in from 1 to 10 years, and they are available in smaller denominations than the bonds.

> **U.S. Treasury notes (T-notes)** Treasury securities that mature in 1 to 10 years.

United States Treasury Bills

The U.S. Treasury issues Treasury bills or T-bills that mature in periods up to 365 days. T-bills pay no cash interest at all during their life. Rather, investors purchase T-bills at a discount from face value, and interest accrues through redemption. At maturity, the U.S. Treasury redeems T-bills at face value. All of the same terms and conditions that apply to T-bonds and T-notes apply to T-bills. The interest is subject to Federal income tax but is exempt from state and local income taxes. T-bills are essentially a highly liquid money market security and represent a place to park large sums of money for a few days, weeks, or months while awaiting the next investment opportunity. Since T-bills trade in the secondary market, investors can buy and sell these instruments almost every day through a stockbroker. Typically the *commission* is approximately $50 per transaction.

> **commission** fee charged by one person/entity to act on behalf of another. Your broker charges you a commission to execute a trade, just as the real estate agent charges you a commission when you buy a house.

These three categories of governments are certainly low-risk investments and could easily be the only thing a person with little or no risk tolerance would own. The shorter the tenor (life of the security), the lower the risk regarding inflation.

U.S. Government Agency Securities

In addition to the direct obligations of the federal government there are a host of government agency securities which are backed by the moral obligation of the Treasury. Such obligation has never been breached to our knowledge.

Names like "Ginnie Mae," "Fannie Mae," "Freddie Mac," "Sallie Mae, and the like, although the subject of another book on fixed-income securities, represent obligations of various federal agencies, but are not all backed by the full faith and credit of the U.S. government:

✔ "Ginnie Mae"—Government National Mortgage Association (GNMA).

✔ "Fannie Mae"—Federal National Mortgage Association (FNMA).

✔ "Freddie Mac"—Federal Home Loan Mortgage Corporation (FHLMC).

✔ "Sallie Mae"—Student Loan Marketing Association (SLMA).

These instruments would be logical choices for a diversified portfolio of low-risk/no-risk securities. To keep the risk as low as possible, such investments would be held to maturity. This would eliminate market risk, especially when you redeem these instruments at maturity at face value. You can accumulate semi-annual interest coupons for later reinvestment or spend the money.

MONEY MARKET MUTUAL FUNDS

Money market mutual funds are basically a portfolio of money market securities. *Money market securities* have a very short term to maturity, generally 270 days or less, are extremely liquid, and carry relatively low risk. A money market mutual fund might invest in:

✔ Commercial paper.
✔ Banker's acceptances.
✔ Repurchase agreements.
✔ Treasury bills.
✔ Certificates of deposit (CDs).

money market securities have a short term to maturity, generally 270 days or less, are extremely liquid, and carry relatively low risk.

Money market mutual funds provide current income to the fund holders and are designed to be extremely safe and conservative. Since these instruments mature in a relatively short period of time, their market values tend to be relatively stable; the market value of a given money market instrument that is sold at par or face value tends to remain the same until maturity. Since the securities in a money market portfolio generally mature within 270 days, the portfolio manager continually buys new securities as existing holdings mature. As such, these funds pay interest income that reflects current market interest rates. These funds reflect changes in short-term interest rates relatively quickly. The share prices of these mutual funds are usually quoted at $1 per share and are designed for those who don't want to sustain any loss of capital.

CERTIFICATES OF DEPOSIT

Certificates of deposit are known as bank CDs. A *certificate of deposit (CD)* is, in effect, a loan made by an individual or institution to a bank. CDs have a fixed term and carry a fixed rate of interest that is determined when opened. Some institutions offer more innovative financial products that tie the CDs' return to another index or government security; however, these instruments do not trade on a stock exchange like a stock or bond. A popular product is a CD whose return is tied to the return of the S&P 500 Index. The interest for the life of the CD and the face amount are returned by the bank at maturity, and can be reinvested or invested elsewhere. CDs' interest is taxable at the federal, state, and local level.

certificate of deposit (CD)   loan made by an individual to a bank.

In order to lower the risk factor even further, making your CDs virtually riskless, diversify (spread out) your investments among several institutions, putting only those amounts that would be fully Federal Deposit Insurance Corporation (FDIC) insured in each bank. Currently, the FDIC insures $100,000 per name per institution. Check the financial institution's credit rating (financial strength) and review the current FDIC rules to make sure that all of your money is insured.

For example, invest $100,000 in a CD offered by bank A, $100,000 in bank B, and $25,000 each in banks C and D. Under this strategy, all of your moneys fall within the $100,000 FDIC-insured limit at each institution. Now, even if all four institutions default on the CDs, your entire $250,000 allocated into CDs would be insured by the FDIC.

MONEY MARKET CERTIFICATES

Money market certificates are basically a certificate representing participation in a portfolio of money market instruments at a bank or other financial institution. Your dollars join those other liquid assets that are waiting for a higher yielding or growth opportunity to present itself to you and could be used interchangeably with individual CDs. Often brokerage houses and nonbank financial institutions offer money market Certificates and CDs that pay higher yields than those CDs offered by commercial banks. Be sure to check the market yields and credit quality of the issuers.

money market certificates represent participation in a portfolio of money market instruments at a bank or other financial institution.

PASSBOOK SAVINGS ACCOUNTS

As was the case with bank CDs, we want to first learn the limits of FDIC insurance available, account by account, at the bank into which we are depositing these savings. With the passbook savings account rates at 2 percent, 3 percent and 4 percent as this book goes to press, you should not consider these accounts to be investment dollars and if the alternative is an insured bank money market account at the same bank at a higher rate with check writing attached, consider that program instead.

SERIES EE & HH UNITED STATES SAVINGS BONDS

Remember when your aunt or grandparents gave you a bond for that birthday, graduation, or other event? Someone paid $25 for a savings bond that eventually was worth $50. Perhaps you authorized payroll deductions for U.S. savings bonds; those weekly deductions came back to you in the form of savings bonds in the following month's pay envelope. These are those loans made to the federal government, guaranteed by the government's full faith and credit—its ability to tax the people and print money. The interest income is free from state and local income taxes. Typically, the U.S. Treasury issues savings bonds in denominations (face value) from $50 to $10,000. Purchasers buy these instruments at half of face value. Savings bonds can accrue interest for as long as 30 years. Series EE bonds aren't marketable, and you get the interest when you redeem them at any time after six months from the day of purchase. That interest is earned every month.

Some versions of EE bonds have their interest rate tracking 90 percent of the five-year Treasury rates. As mentioned above, interest on EE bonds is free from state and local income taxes and can even be totally tax-free if you use the proceeds for educational purposes under the guidelines. A form to purchase such bonds is available at your local bank along with a chart of the various income levels that would qualify you to enjoy that tax free status when you use the proceeds from savings bonds for education. There are income restrictions on this benefit, so consult your tax adviser or financial planner.

Series HH bonds carry the same guarantee, are issued by the U.S. Treasury, and have the same tax benefits and other features as their EE cousins with the following exceptions: HH bonds pay interest on a semiannual basis and are usually held for a shorter term. You can roll your EE bonds into HH bonds and continue to enjoy the tax-deferred status you enjoyed before.

In order to obtain the latest rate information on savings bonds, use the following toll-free number: 1-800-4US-BOND (1-800-487-2663). Or, access the Internet for the Bureau of Public Debt Web site: www.savbonds@bpd.treas.gov.

When you access the Web site, you can find:

✔ Press releases.

✔ Current interest rates.

✔ Information on buying and redeeming bonds.

✔ Answers to frequently asked questions about savings bonds.

✔ Answers to frequently asked questions about taxes.

✔ Bond pricing tools.

✔ Savings Bonds Wizard (question and answers).

✔ Forms for savings bonds transactions.

INFLATION-INDEXED TREASURY BONDS

These instruments carry the same benefits as the other U.S. Treasury securities described in this chapter, but the interest payments are adjusted annually for inflation. These securities are designed to protect your purchasing power and provide the safety of a conservative, high-quality fixed-income investment.

LIFE INSURANCE

For the purposes of this section, we'll first touch on insurance you already own and then give you a formula for determining how much life insurance you should own.

Ask you insurance adviser how much *cash value* you have in the typical *whole-life* policy or policies you own. Most of you reading this book probably own some portfolio of whole-life insurance that has been held for 8 to 10 years or more and you have built up some cash value/idle equity. If the policies you hold at present have sufficient cash value to continue the premium payments without you paying additional premiums, consider instructing your agent or insurance professional to use that cash value for that purpose.

> **cash value**   the dollars built up in an insurance policy from dividends earned or investments made by the issuer. Cash value can be borrowed from yourself and has the effect of lowering the death benefit on the policy. The older the policy, the greater the amount of cash value available. Term insurance doesn't build cash value, but just provides coverage.

When you implement this strategy, you are borrowing against the equity in the policy and reducing the face value of the policy. As a result, upon your death your heirs will receive a smaller benefit. In connection with this plan, you may want to use some of those dollars you were previously channeling toward paying the whole-life premiums to buy small *term insurance* policies to make up the face value shortfall. Once you have put that idle equity to use paying the premiums, you can turn those dollars around to purchase the additional coverage you need for your family's protection. Notice we didn't use the word "investment" in that last sentence, but rather the words "coverage" and "protection". You own insurance policies to protect you and your family and cover you against the unforeseen events that you do not have the financial power or wherewithal to handle. You should allocate other moneys to make investments to realize income and gains.

> **whole-life**   a type of insurance coverage that builds up a cash value from the premiums paid and the financial success of the insurance company, as opposed to term insurance, which provides only a death benefit. The cash value in a whole-life insurance policy can be borrowed out and repaid later, while such a feature isn't part of a term policy.

> **term insurance**   simple coverage that provides a death benefit and builds up no cash value. Term is usually the least expensive form of life insurance and can be bought in large amounts at a relatively cheap price to provide coverage for young, growing families.

How much insurance coverage/protection does that typical 40- to 45-year-old head of a family with two kids, a mortgage, car payments, student loans, credit card debt, home improvement loans, and all the rest of a typical family's financial responsibilities need? The following formula is suggested:

✔ Three times the gross family income (both husband and wife, interest dividends, etc.).

✔ Amount of the gross family debt (mortgages, student loans, car loans, home improvement loans, credit cards, a relative's advance as the down payment on the house).

✔ Between $50,000 and $100,000 to cover extra expenses such as your final expenses (cost of funeral and burial) plus money to cover your family's transition expenses to ease their loss.

Add the above figures together. The result is your insurance needs, which probably total many hundreds of thousands of dollars. This is the amount of life insurance the principal breadwinner in your household should carry. These policies should be payable to the non-principal bread-winner. In other words, your spouse or partner should be the named beneficiary on the policy. It is worthwhile to review your policies every year or two and whenever you have a major family change. Also meet with your family attorney, tax adviser, or financial planner to determine whether an insurance trust would help you and your family reduce the burden of estate taxes.

The non-principal breadwinner should carry another life insurance policy in the amount $100,000 or more. The beneficiary under this policy should be the principal breadwinner. Why?

Let's consider the traditional husband-and-wife family model where one spouse is the primary breadwinner and the other spouse runs the household. In today's world, this could be either the man or the woman. Under this scenario, were the primary breadwinner to die, the surviving spouse should receive enough insurance coverage/protection to either re-pay all of the family debt or continue to service that debt and enjoy three years of income to live on while he or she gets his or her life back in order. On the other hand, should the nonbreadwinner spouse die, the breadwin-ner still can continue working and earn his or her income and could use the $100,000 insurance benefits to cover child care for a number of years while he or she gets his or her life back together.

Whether all of this new coverage is whole-life, term life insurance, or any other sort of plan is based on your family's ability to pay the premiums while the coverage is needed. The amount of coverage will probably decline as your family income becomes more stable; your net worth increases; the children grow up, are educated, and move out of the house; and family debt is reduced. Not having this coverage/protection means assuming a high de-gree of risk—most likely more risk than you can afford to assume.

OTHER INSURANCE (NONLIFE)

In conjunction with life insurance coverage, for similar reasons, it is nec-essary to protect your family from unforeseen losses resulting from fire, theft, storms, loss of income, and so on. Consider the following types of insurance coverage.

To do this properly, you may want to engage an insurance consultant to set it all up. You may want an insurance planner or in some cases a CLU (char-tered life underwriter) to establish an overall insurance plan, using some of the components discussed here. After you create a plan, implement it.

Property and Casualty Insurance

Most of the readers of this book own either a home, a condo or a co-op, rent an apartment or townhouse, or otherwise have a place full of family stuff to live in. That is what this type of insurance is protecting. In the event of a fire, property and casualty insurance protects your dwelling and your belongings. Read your policies carefully to make sure you have adequate coverage. Make sure the dollar or face value of your policy is high enough to meet your needs and that the articles you need covered are in fact covered by the policy.

For example, if you have a home office, the typical homeowner's policy does not cover losses to the home office. If you have extensive computer equipment or other valuables such as furs or jewelry in your home, your homeowners' policy probably does not cover these losses. You may want to purchase a rider or endorsement that provides coverage for these specific items.

Add up the replacement value (remember to add an inflation factor of 4 percent to 7 percent per year to these numbers) of your home and your belongings, including the home itself and a reasonable number representing liability. For example, if you have a swimming pool or other so-called attractive nuisances, this amount should be higher. You may want to purchase an umbrella liability policy. The sum of these amounts is the amount of property and casualty coverage you should carry.

You may want to pay these and other insurance premiums annually to reduce the cost of the premiums. If you need relatively low-cost funds, consider using a home equity line of credit to get a lower premium and then repay the home equity loan (yourself) monthly. This would have the effect of making all those insurance premiums a tax-advantaged expense.

Disability Insurance

Statistics show that it is more likely that a family will lose their home due to disability than to death. Disability insurance will provide income at the rate of approximately 60 percent of your working income. Remember, if you are disabled your expenses are likely to be lower and the 60 percent replacement factor is net of income taxes while your salary was a pretax amount. In general, when you pay the disability insurance premiums with after-tax dollars, any benefits you receive are in after-tax dollars. In the event your employer provides this coverage and pays the premiums, any benefits you receive would be taxable to you. Disability insurance provides no investment buildup. Disability insurance allows you to be home for a period of time and continue to support your family.

It is important to determine what your policy covers. There are several key features of disability policies that will help you in the event you become disabled and are unable to continue your present job. First, exactly what constitutes disability in the eyes of the insurance company? In other words, would the insurance company pay benefits in the event you cannot perform any job or in the event you are unable to perform your current job? Is the policy portable? In other words, if you leave your current employer, can you take your disability policy with you? How much of your working income will you receive on a monthly basis? This is called the replacement ratio. When would your benefits begin? This is called the waiting period and means the amount of time you have to be out of work before you begin collecting benefits. This period is typically 180 days. When you wait 180 days before collecting benefits, your premiums would be less than if your waiting period were only 90 days. This is similar to a deductible. Also, would you be entitled to cost-of-living allowance (COLA) adjustments? Most policies offer a defined benefit—a fixed amount of money equal to 60 percent of your salary income—and you receive that amount once you become disabled and meet the waiting period and other requirements designated in your policy; however, once you begin receiving benefits, the insurance company will increase those benefits every year in relation to the inflation rate.

INSURANCE RISK

Typically, you should consider insurance as a long-term investment. Insurance as an asset allocation tool should be placed into the low-risk basket. Insurance serves to protect your income and your wealth. Since people pay insurance premiums every year, year in, year out, and don't know when, if ever, they will need the benefits, it is crucial to select an insurer or insurance company that carries the highest credit rating. Many people purchase insurance based on price. In other words, they purchase the policy that charges the lowest premium. This price trade-off may not be worthwhile if the insurer goes bankrupt and cannot pay your benefits when you most need the money. Visit your public library and review the A. M. Best Company reports to determine the financial strength of the insurance companies from which you buy or are considering buying policies.

UMBRELLA LIABILITY COVERAGE

Umbrella liability coverage provides protection in case someone gets injured by you at your home or when you are driving and sues you. If the limit of the amount of liability coverage afforded by your homeowner's policy is $100,000 and a neighbor's kid slips on your patio, falls into your empty swimming pool, and gets hurt, count on being sued for many times that amount. The same type of liability exists with your car. If you lose a claim in amounts above the liability coverage you carry, you will be obligated to pay the difference from the rest of your assets.

To calculate just how much of an umbrella you need, calculate the sum of all of your assets and then subtract the amount of liability coverage you carry presently. Take the smallest amount of coverage from among all of your policies, unless all of your policies carry the same amount. The result of this calculation is the amount of umbrella insurance you need. Should you lose that case and the settlement is in the millions, the first $100,000 or $200,000 or total liability coverage of the policy in question is paid by the insurance company and the rest is covered by the umbrella policy up to the policy limit. Many umbrella liability policies offer $1 million to $2 million of coverage and have a $300,000 deductible (which amount should be the amount of coverage under your automobile or homeowner's policy). Make sure that the coverage under the umbrella policy picks up where the other policies stop.

Several million dollars of coverage may sound like an expensive purchase, but such coverage costs only a few hundred dollars per year, all things being equal—your age, location, and so on. In many ways, this coverage may be the most important protection you buy in your lifetime. This policy could protect your home, stock portfolio, and other assets from loss.

CASH UNDER THE MATTRESS/IN THE VAULT

Cash on hand or under the mattress is simply extra spending money or emergency money. Keep in mind that cash in the mattress or in the vault is 100 percent idle equity, earns nothing, doesn't grow, and loses buying power day by day. With cash on hand, you are failing to take advantage of other investment opportunities that may come along from time to time. The cost of such cash is huge. With today's technology, you can visit an ATM (automated teller machine) almost anywhere in the world and withdraw cash from your checking or savings account, and you can use a credit card in just the same way. You could store some traveler's checks in your home. They have the equivalent liquidity of cash, but generally, you can recover your money in the event someone steals your traveler's checks.

If, in order to have peace of mind and have the "sleep well at night" factor we spoke of in Chapter 3, knowing that a few thousand dollars or more is on hand to grab at any time gives you a sense of security, then that is the cost of such security. You know the cost, you accept the cost, and in return you get the comfort. Is it so silly that no one does it? Will your friends and neighbors tell you you're crazy to have a few bucks in the mattress? Or are they doing the same thing? You have more company than you know, but don't overdo it. A few weeks' gross expenses in the cookie jar is okay. But more than that should be invested somewhere where that money will produce income or grow and could be borrowed against in an emergency.

Whether that cash is put into the mattress or into a money market account, passbook savings account, or wherever, the only way you will ever have enough wealth to do whatever you want to do is to invest to realize your goals and dreams.

OPTIONS

Options are a form of derivatives; *options* represent contracts to buy or sell a specific security or commodity at a specific price within a specified period of time. For example, a Procter & Gamble Corporation January 80 call option gives the holder the right but not the obligation to purchase from the person who wrote the option 100 shares of Procter & Gamble common stock at $80 per share (the *exercise price* or strike price) at any time between now and the expiration date. The expiration date would be the third Saturday of the month of January. The holder of this option would pay the *writer* of the option a premium, similar to an insurance premium, for this right. The premium depends on how much time there is between now and January, the current market price of Procter & Gamble common stock in relation to the $80 strike price, and the volatility of Procter & Gamble's common stock.

options the right or privilege (but not the obligation) to buy (for a call) or sell (for a put) something in the future.

exercise price   in the world of options, the fixed price the owner of an option has the right to pay to (for a call) or demand from (for a put) the seller or grantor for the underlying stock over the life of the option. Same as the strike price.

writer   the one who sells an option and stands ready to sell the stock in question, if a call option was written, or purchase the stock in question if a put option was written. The writer is often known as the grantor of the option.

Put options give the holder the right to sell a specific stock within a specific period of time at a specific price to the writer of the put option.

put   an option that allows the owner to sell the underlying security to the seller/grantor of the option at a fixed price for a fixed period of time. Puts are usually purchased in anticipation of a declining market to lock in as much of the current value as possible.

The purchase of an option, whether it is a put or call option, represents 100 percent risk, as the option is likely to expire worthless. When an option expires worthless (e.g., you do not *exercise* the option), you will lose your entire purchase price (premium). The sale of an option, whether it is a put or a call option, without owning the underlying security (being naked), represents unlimited risk, as the stock's price can move significantly in the opposite direction from your option.

For example, if you sell that Procter & Gamble $80 call, you are collecting the premium and giving the holder the right to buy 100 shares of Procter & Gamble common stock from you at $80 until the January expiration date. If you don't already own 100 shares of Procter & Gamble common stock, the call is considered to be naked. Suppose the price of Procter & Gamble common stock jumps to $95; the holder of the call option would certainly want to exercise the option and purchase Procter & Gamble common stock for $80 per share. If you don't own Procter & Gamble common stock and your call gets exercised, you would have to go into the open market and purchase 100 shares of Procter & Gamble common stock at $95 and sell those shares for $80 per share. Of course, you would keep the call premium which may have been $3 to $4 per share. *When you write naked options, your losses could be infinite.*

> **exercise** the holder of a put or call option can choose to exercise the option. In the case of a call option, the holder calls the stock away from the writer and buys the shares of the common stock at the option strike price. In the case of a put option, the holder puts the stock to the writer and sells the shares of common stock at the option strike price.

On the other hand, if you are the *grantor* (seller) of an option and you own the underlying security, you can be said to be at no risk at all. In this case, you would be considered to be covered. If you have 100 shares of Procter & Gamble common stock and sell that January $80 call, you would keep the premium and receive $80 per share, or $8000 minus commissions, if Procter & Gamble common stock trades above $80 just before the option expires. This covered call writing transaction is relatively low-risk. The main risk with this strategy is that you effectively cap your upside to $80 (the strike price) plus the call premium ($3 to $4 in this example) minus commissions. Many investors write covered calls to generate current income from their portfolio.

> **grantor** in the world of options, the seller of an option and the one who stands ready either to sell the underlying stock in the case of granting a call option or to buy the underlying stock back in the case of the grantor of a put option.

For example, suppose you own a stock at a gain (unrealized gain). You want to protect or lock in your gain, so you place a good till canceled *stop-loss order* under the current value of the stock—perhaps 7 percent to

10 percent below the current market price. At the same time, you decide to sell an out-of-the-money covered call against the stock you own. For that Procter & Gamble common stock, suppose the current market price equals $65. Perhaps you set a stop-loss order at $55. If the market price of Procter & Gamble common stock hits $55, then your *limit order* becomes a market order and your broker would sell your shares at the next market bid. At the same time, suppose you sell a January $75 call; you might collect a call premium of $3 minus commissions. With this strategy, you place yourself in a win-win-win situation because it doesn't matter which way the stock goes—you make money if the stock increases in value, if it decreases in value, and if its value stays the same.

stop-loss order   an order to buy or sell a security at a limit price. When the market price reaches the limit price, your order becomes a market order and is executed on the next sale. You would place a stop-loss order to limit your loss on an investment. Suppose you purchased 100 shares of ABC Company common stock for $40 per share and you don't want to lose more than $4 per share or 10 percent of your investment; you would place a stop-loss order with your broker-dealer.

limit order   an order to buy or sell a security at a specific price. Once the market price hits the limit, the trade would be executed as long as there is no stock ahead of you.

If the price of Procter & Gamble common stock rises above the $75 strike price, the option holder calls (buys) your Procter & Gamble stock. The call option holder calls the stock away from you at the strike price and you keep the premium you received when you granted the option.

If the stock goes sideways, the option expires unexercised, so you keep the premium you received when you granted the option, you still own the stock with the built-in unrealized gain, you continue receiving the stock's dividends, and you can sell another covered call option.

If the stock goes down, the option expires worthless, so you keep the premium you received when you sold the option, your stop-loss order takes you out at that earlier locked-in gain, with the proceeds available for reinvestment, and you win again. The drawback with this scenario is that stocks tend to be volatile and you may trigger the stop-loss order due to a temporary decline in the stock price. While this protects your gain, you would owe income taxes on the capital gain and you may miss out on the future appreciation.

DIAMONDS AND SPIDERS

These aren't precious gems or crawling creatures that give many people arachnophobia, but rather investment vehicles that need to be considered at all risk levels.

DIAMONDS^{SM} are a derivative security created by the brokerage community that allows you to own an interest in all 30 components of the Dow Jones Industrial Index, in the form of a trust. The DIAMONDS trust moves in value in direct proportion to the Dow Jones Industrial Average itself. If the Dow goes up 3 percent in value, DIAMONDS would be worth approximately 3 percent more, and if the Dow drops, shares of DIA-MONDS drop in direct proportion. You can buy DIAMONDS the same way you buy 100 shares of a stock, place a stop-loss order under their current value and even buy them on margin. With a 100-share purchase, you own an interest in all 30 stocks in the Dow Jones Industrial Average. From the standpoint of low risk you are really invested in a portfolio of the bluest of the blue chips and have a part of the fabric of corporate America in your portfolio.

We include DIAMONDS in this low-risk assets category because when you consider the quality of stocks like Eastman Kodak, IBM, Procter & Gamble, and DuPont, to mention just a few, you're talking about multibillion-dollar, global companies, household names. These companies have been paying quarterly dividends for decades and their shares are included in the portfolios of most major institutions in the world.

Spiders are a similar type of derivative security, with the only essential difference being the makeup of the portfolio. Instead of owning an interest in a trust holding the 30 components of the Dow Jones Industrial Average, spiders (really SPDRs—Standard & Poor's Depositary Receipts) are invested into the 500 components of the Standard & Poor's 500 Index. This index represents a much broader cross section of the market/economy and contains shares from the Dow 30 as well as most of the rest of blue-chip corporate America. Spiders trade on the AMEX (the American Stock Exchange). Spiders, in this sense, would have to be considered a low-risk investment.

Just as you can use options to hedge your portfolio, derivative securities can accomplish the same thing. Further discussions of derivatives will be found in both Chapters 6 and 7.

Chapter
6

Medium-Risk Assets

MEDIUM-RISK ASSET CATEGORY EXPLAINED

Medium-risk assets include those investments and investment vehicles that have a reasonable probability they will appreciate in value and that bear a certain degree of risk, but not an astronomical degree of risk. Investors who pursue medium-risk investments tend to possess an average risk tolerance level, have a reasonable understanding of finance and investments, seek capital appreciation (growth), and don't want to risk losing their entire investment. They desire to sleep a little better at night than the highflier who would use mostly high-risk investments.

Medium-risk assets typically would not be subject to wild volatility or wide fluctuation, would offer stable income and predictable dividends, and would move only slightly in response to changes in the economy and market interest rates. As a part of your portfolio aimed at growth, emerging growth and aggressive growth, medium-risk assets would comprise approximately one-third of that segment. As you will note from the examples given, investments in this group are from recognizable sources, do not include new issues or *initial public offerings (IPOs)*, and can often be found in mutual funds.

initial public offering (IPO)   when the company or its investment bankers sell shares of the company's common stock to the public (individual investors) or mutual funds for the first time.

NATURE OF RISK

In Chapter 5, we discussed low-risk assets—those investments that offer relatively stable income and little if any risk to principal, and that stabilize your portfolio or hedge against other risks and exposures. In contrast, medium-risk assets offer the prospect of a blend of income and appreciation. As discussed, with the possibility for appreciation comes the possibility of loss. Medium-risk assets combine potential appreciation and risk of loss in a proportion that should result in reasonable return and relatively low risk compared to high-risk assets.

RISKS WITH MEDIUM-RISK ASSETS

The major risk with the medium-risk asset class is misunderstanding the nature and characteristics of the investment. Very often, investors purchase securities without actually understanding all the hurdles involved in realizing the target upside and without actually understanding all of the risks to their money. A number of investors consider the risks but don't necessarily weigh the probability of those risks actually occurring. The other risk to medium-risk assets is mistaking them for low-risk assets. While this may seem unlikely, many investors purchase different investments over time. Some of these investments overlap as to purpose and the risks inherent in an investment are likely to change over time.

For example, Chapter 5 discussed Treasury securities, which are considered to be among the lowest-risk assets available today. As we extend the tenor or maturity of these U.S. government securities to 10, 20, or 30 years, additional risks materialize. While the U.S. government guarantees the payment of the principal and interest of the Treasury notes and bonds, perhaps the credit rating of the United States will change in that time frame. This occurred in some Asian countries in late 1997 and 1998.

Even if the U.S. government pays the interest income, these payments are fixed amounts of money, so the investor bears inflation risk. And, the longer the tenor, the more the market value of the investment is subject to changes due to changes in market interest rates. So, in this example, we have considered a relatively low-risk investment and changed the terms of the investment. Now we are assuming more risk than we may have initially thought.

PLACE IN PORTFOLIO/PURPOSE

We recommend that medium-risk assets comprise between 35 percent and 80 percent of your portfolio. Please review Chapter 3 and reread the asset allocation models to determine the appropriate division of medium-risk assets in your particular case. Mixing low-risk, medium-risk, and high-risk assets all in the same larger portfolio allows you to diversify your dollars between and among many different kinds of investments and accomplish your financial goals.

Medium-risk assets serve to smooth out your investment portfolio. To achieve a target rate of return, you might invest a portion of your money in low-, medium-, and high-risk assets. Many investors consider medium-risk assets to be the core or base of their portfolio. These investments grow at a relatively reliable and steady pace compared to high-risk assets, are likely to generate a reasonably high level of current income, and fluctuate in value more than low-risk assets and less than high-risk assets.

HEDGING YOUR BETS

The best way to protect your investments and net worth is to make wise investment decisions. This means:

- ✔ Becoming an educated consumer of financial products.
- ✔ Keeping informed about current trends and developments in the financial world.
- ✔ Dealing only with top professionals who are honest people.
- ✔ Getting sound advice on a regular basis and as needed.
- ✔ Diversifying and allocating your assets wisely.
- ✔ Working with sophisticated and knowledgeable peers and mentors.

SPECIAL ADVISERS

Many people get involved in a wide variety of costly investments without getting proper professional advice. We recall numerous cases of individuals who have purchased primary residences and have not hired engineers to inspect the homes. In one case, the house's foundation was faulty, and after the new buyers moved in, half the house sank into the ground and the house was condemned. The cost of a professional home inspection would have been only about $500 and the buyers were still on the hook to repay the mortgage of more than $150,000. Do your homework and invest money up front in order to increase your returns and preserve your wealth.

The more important and expensive the investment, and the bigger percentage of your portfolio the investment represents, the more important it is to seek professional advice. The more specialized and complicated the investment, the more important it is to get specialized professional advice from:

- ✔ CFP—certified financial planner.
- ✔ ChFC—chartered financial consultant.
- ✔ CPA—certified public accountant.
- ✔ Insurance experts and consultants.
- ✔ PE—professional engineer (regarding real estate investments).
- ✔ Lawyers—tax, estate, trust, and certain other family and business matters.
- ✔ Other business consultants.

Even a onetime consultation can help you invest more wisely and establish an asset allocation that will best meet your goals and objectives. Professional fees can yield significant returns. In a concrete way, a consultant can help you establish a financial plan, an insurance program covering all the categories discussed in Chapter 5, a projection of the tax consequences of everything you are doing, and peace of mind, knowing the real estate and other complex investments you hold and are considering are in good condition. By taking advantage of the skills of these professionals, you are further reducing the risk of proceeding with this slice of your investment pizza pie.

DEFERRED ANNUITIES (SINGLE PREMIUM)

We place this product in the medium-risk category and not the low-risk category because annuities are generally designed to bear some risk on a relative basis. Annuities bear credit risk, tax risk, legal risk, relatively high expenses, and market risk.

There are two basic types of annuity products to consider: fixed annuities and variable annuities. In addition, there are even more choices between and among the insurance companies issuing such products.

Fixed Annuities

With a fixed annuity, after you have paid that single onetime premium, the insurance company will promise you a minimum return on those dollars on a tax-deferred basis. The actual return on investment may or may not exceed the minimum rate. A *fixed annuity* that pays a (minimum) fixed rate of return represents a credit obligation of the party promising to make the annuity payment stream. When the interest rate or rate of return is a fixed rate, this may or may not provide protection against inflation. Other investments may have more potential to increase in value over time.

> **fixed annuity**   pays a (minimum) fixed rate of return, and represents a credit obligation of the party (usually an insurance company) promising to make the annuity payment stream.

To the extent the annuity's historical returns have exceeded the annuity's guaranteed minimum rate of return, these higher rates may not be realized in the future. To be conservative, you should assume that the annuity will compound (yield) at the minimum guaranteed rate of return only. Any extra yield will be a bonus and will increase your wealth. Second, the quality of the annuity is only as high as the quality of the sponsor and the securities that comprise the investment portfolio. The annuity's prospectus should contain the annuity's investment policies. Select only sponsors of the highest quality.

Variable Annuities

In the case of a *variable annuity*, the portfolio manager invests your dollars in instruments that can vary in value. Variable annuities typically invest their funds in a portfolio of common stocks such as the S&P 500 Index. These annuities do promise a minimum rate of return, but that may be all you get.

> **variable annuity**   annuity in which the portfolio manager invests your dollars in instruments that can vary in value (there is a minimum rate of return).

OTHER CONSIDERATIONS WITH ANNUITIES

Financial Strength

The rating or ranking or financial stability of the insurance company or annuity sponsor presents yet another risk factor that puts this class into the medium category. Review the A. M. Best reports in your local public library or on the Internet. These reports will reveal whether the company is highly rated or poorly rated. That rating should be given considerable weight. Stick with insurance companies and annuity sponsors that are of the highest credit quality and financial quality. If the insurance company is highly rated and the track record is good in that they have been returning higher dollar amounts over an extended period of time, you might consider this product for your medium-risk asset category.

Tax Advantages

Many people invest in annuities because the investment income is tax-deferred until you make withdrawals. This can be an effective way to build wealth for retirement. However, today many employees can take advantage of employer-sponsored retirement programs, such as 401(k) and 403(b) plans, and IRAs. Often these plans are less expensive than annuities. Also, before investing in an annuity, you should evaluate the Roth IRA.

Expenses

Fees and other costs are an important consideration when choosing an annuity. An annuity is the combination of an investment and an insurance product. The investment component of the annuity is similar to a mutual fund and the sponsor charges investment and management fees and expenses. The insurance component is central to the annuity since the insurance policy enables the portfolio earnings to accumulate tax-deferred until the holder makes withdrawals.

Single Premium versus Periodic Payment Annuities

Under a single premium or lump sum annuity, the annuity holder makes one single payment at the beginning of the annuity policy. The portfolio should grow over time. When the holder wants to begin making withdrawals, the sponsor annuitizes the value of your account and establishes a periodic payment stream over your life expectancy. Under a periodic payment annuity, the holder invests money every month or every quarter and the holder's portfolio should grow over time based on investment returns and each periodic investment.

YOUR HOME (PRIMARY RESIDENCE/VACATION HOME)

For most of you reading this book, your home represents your biggest asset. We authors will not tell you where to live, how to live, what style of house to live in, or even how much to spend on real estate. Rather, we recognize that most of you will own real property.

A number of people own seasonal or vacation homes. This is a luxury and can be quite enjoyable, especially if the home is located in an area you enjoy and your visits provide you with a change of scenery from your daily environment. In our experience, a vacation home has not been an excellent investment from a financial point of view. We have worked with some people who have found an area that they enjoy and have decided to purchase a vacation home with the intention of retiring to that home in the future. This strategy has worked for a number of people. The value of a vacation home depends on the location; the proximity to activities such as skiing, hiking, boating, and so on; the style and size of the home; and the economy.

Home ownership typically provides a certain amount of tax benefits. Interest on mortgages and home equity loans and lines of credit are deductible on primary and secondary homes (two homes in total) up to $1 million in loan principal. Generally, property and school taxes are also tax-deductible. The taxpayer has to itemize deductions on his or her income tax return (complete Schedule A on Form 1040 of the Internal Revenue Service). It is worthwhile to meet with your tax adviser to discuss the value of the tax deductions to you. Over time, the IRS has reduced the amount of tax deductions individuals can take based on their income levels. Higher-income earners risk having their deductions disallowed and they may face the alternative minimum tax.

Owning real property is no guarantee that its value will always go up, much less keep pace with inflation. Few parts of the country have enjoyed uninterrupted increases in real estate values, and in some cases property values have fallen. When industry moves into the area, an airport is built in the next county, the new interstate doesn't have an exit into your community, the schools are falling apart, while the tax base is eroding, property values are likely to drop. Given these few examples, the average person should consider real estate as something to live in and enjoy and maybe get some tax benefits from, but not necessarily make a significant amount of money on.

As a general rule, you should have a principal residence and maybe a vacation home whose cost would be calculated by taking the dollars you have available as a down payment and adding:

✔ To be conservative, a mortgage equal to one year's gross income.

✔ To be less conservative, a mortgage equal to one and one-half years' gross income.

✔ To be living a little on the edge, a mortgage equal to two or more years' gross income.

These rules of thumb assume that you owe no other debt. If you have a car loan, student loans, credit card debt, home improvement loans, consumer loans, family loans, and so on, your gross family debt including those mortgages should be within the above guidelines to be able to re-duce your financial risk.

There is nothing wrong with owning your house outright—free and clear of debt—even though:

You lose the tax deduction you were enjoying from paying interest on that mortgage.

You also have several hundred thousand dollars of idle equity that could be invested elsewhere tied up in that house.

This may seem like a contrarian approach, and your friends, neigh-bors, financial advisers, and tax professionals may tell you that you are crazy. However, by owning that house outright, you will be paying less "rent" every month.

You will have more dollars every month or year to spend or reinvest.

You will sleep better at night knowing that no one can come and take your home away from you.

You will have that peace of mind that transcends dollars.

All of these points apply to either your principal residence or one va-cation property, or to a combination of the two. Together, these two resi-dences count as your home. With certain limitations, you can deduct the property taxes, and mortgage interest, enjoy the tax-deferred appreciation and pay no capital gains taxes on the first $500,000 of those gains, for a married couple, if you live in these residences for two years before selling.

LONG-TERM GOVERNMENT BONDS

Since we have already touched on government securities in Chapter 5, we will confine our remarks in this section to just long-term (10 years or longer) United States Treasury bonds and other long-term United States government agency securities.

Even though Treasuries and agency securities carry either the full faith and credit or moral obligation of the U.S. Treasury as security and will pay full face value at maturity unless the global economy comes crashing down on our heads, we consider such issues to fit into the medium-risk category because of the following risk factors:

✔ You may need to sell those bonds before maturity and may or may not get full face value, depending on the interest rate market at the time you have to sell. As we discussed earlier, the market value of a bond (especially a long-term bond) fluctuates inversely to market interest rates.

✔ Since these obligations return a fixed amount of interest, you may suffer loss of buying power over time, especially since the holding period of these bonds could span decades.

✔ In the case of government agency securities that don't enjoy the full faith and credit backing of the U.S. Treasury, but are just senior unsecured obligations, it is possible (although of relatively low probability) that a default could occur.

In any event, if you need access to the money before maturity, you could always *margin* your securities. Margin means borrowing money against the market value of your securities. Current rules allow investors to borrow up to 90 percent of market value of U.S. Treasury and U.S. agency securities. You can use the money for other purposes and hold the bonds until maturity, thereby avoiding having to sell the bonds below face value and incur commissions and taxes. While the legal margin limit is 90 percent, you leave yourself a much greater cushion by borrowing only 30 percent to 40 percent of the market value of your securities. By following this strategy, you protect yourself in the event of a market decline and should avoid a margin call.

margin   money borrowed to purchased securities.

TAX-EXEMPT MUNICIPAL BONDS (MUNIS)

Many people place municipal bonds in the low-risk category. After all, they are backed by the issuing municipality and that town isn't likely to go out of business. The reason we place munis in the medium-risk category is because often a closer examination of the following will reveal something more than low or no risk.

- ✔ Quality of the community: demographics.
- ✔ Stability and breadth of the industry base.
- ✔ Strength of the local economy.
- ✔ Tenor (life) of the bond.

General obligation (G.O.) bonds are backed by the full faith and credit of the issuer. General obligation bonds issued by a huge city with a large tax base and substantial industry, insured and rated AAA or Aaa by the top rating agencies, and held to maturity could be considered to be riskless except for the loss of buying power over time. It is all the other billions of dollars' worth of outstanding munis that need our attention here.

Bonds with a lower than investment-grade rating are considered to be more risky. Investors bear greater risk of losing their coupon and principal. Here are the top four credit ratings from the two major credit rating services:

Standard & Poor's	Moody's Investors Service
AAA	Aaa
AA	Aa
A	A
BBB	Baa

Bonds with these four ratings are considered *investment-grade bonds*. Anything below is considered to be noninvestment-grade and subjects you to more risk the further down the rating spectrum you go. To own bonds rated below these four levels would be to subject yourself to the risk of a less stable community, a smaller tax base, or smaller revenues from that sewer project as well as the questionable ability of the issuer to repay the principal at maturity.

> **investment-grade bonds**   bonds rated among the top four categories by the major rating services.

Revenue bonds and notes are backed by the revenue from a specific project such as a bridge or tunnel. Owning revenue type munis rather than general obligation bonds raises the risk of insufficient tolls being collected on that highway that the bonds financed or lower sewer hookup charges for that sewer plant built in that smaller community. Revenue bonds depend on the revenues from the project built with the money raised and not the ability of the community to levy property taxes. Revenue bonds generally command higher yields than general obligation bonds because they generally carry a higher level of risk.

It is important to calculate whether your net yield is higher with a muni than a taxable bond of the same quality. If a bond pays 7 percent and your income tax rate equals 30 percent, for every $70 in interest income you earn, you would pay $21 in income taxes and retain $49 in after-tax interest income. If you invest in a triple-tax-free bond that yields 5 percent, a $1000 bond would pay $50 in interest income. Since your effective income tax rate on that bond equals zero, you would pay no income taxes. For every $1 you earn in interest income, you keep $1. In this example, given these assumptions and if the credit quality is the same for both bonds, the after-tax return on the muni exceeds the that of the taxable bond. Compute your net after-tax rate of return before you invest in municipal securities.

COVERED CALL OPTIONS

The subject of options frightens many seasoned investors and certainly the novice. The authors are not suggesting that options are for everyone. Rather, we urge every investor to at least become familiar with the terms and language, know the risk factors involved with options, and understand how the options markets work.

In Chapter 5, we mentioned the use of options from the standpoint of you as the buyer of puts and calls. In this chapter we discuss options from the standpoint of you as the grantor or writer of covered options.

We have already learned in Chapter 5 that simply buying put or call options can represent 100 percent risk, since if the option is allowed to expire unexercised, you lose the entire purchase price (premium) of that put or call. On the other hand, you also learned in that same chapter that the grantor (seller) of an option is in a different position, since the seller gets the premium and if the option were to expire unexercised the seller would keep the premium and can then sell another option.

An advantageous position is to be a covered call writer.

Covered call means that you already own the underlying stock and you are selling a call against that common stock in order to earn current income. In the event that the market price of the stock exceeds the option strike price on the expiration date, the option holder will buy or call your common stock. Since you already own the common stock, you are considered to be covered and if the option holder calls your stock, you don't have to enter the market to purchase the stock just called from you. In this way, if you sell call options where the option strike price exceeds the current market value of the stock when you sell or write the option, you are creating a potential winning position. If the stock appreciates beyond the option strike price by the expiration date and you don't redeem (buy back) your option or roll it out to another expiration, then you would retain the call premium plus the sales proceeds (the strike price multiplied by the number of shares, less commissions).

> **covered call**   an investor holds 100 shares of common stock and sells a call. The call option is said to be covered because the writer of the call option owns shares of the underlying common stock.

Writing covered call options has the effect of lowering your cost basis on the stock. Suppose you purchase 100 shares of Procter & Gamble common stock for $80. Your investment or basis in the stock would equal $8000 (100 shares multiplied by $80 per share) plus commissions. Next, you sell a covered call option that expires three months from now and has a strike price of $85. This call premium may equal $3 per share or $300 in total (minus commissions). You collect the proceeds from selling the call option the trading day after you sell the option. Now, your cost per share, ignoring commissions, equals $77 ($80 purchase price per share minus $3 call option premium collected).

We place covered call writing into the medium-risk category when selling calls on medium-risk stocks. Options are derivatives, since they derive their value from the underlying asset. In the case of a call option (for example, put vs. call), the option derives its value from the market value of the underlying stock in relation to the option strike price and the time until expiration. Also, the volatility of the underlying common stock has a direct effect on the value of the call option.

If viewed from the standpoint of writing calls against stocks already owned, but at a gain, you could move such an event from medium risk to low risk. As described earlier, if a stock is owned at a gain and that gain is protected by a stop-loss order and you write a covered call option, the grantor of the covered call could be said to be in a win-win-win situation. You would make money regardless of whether the stock goes up, goes down or continues to move sideways. Reread the end of Chapter 5 and learn how you can position yourself to win.

REAL ESTATE

The security and comfort offered by the terms "triple net lease," "all cash," and "low leverage" would under ordinary circumstances give you the impression that these deals are foolproof and should be considered in the low-risk group. This is especially so if the major tenants are well-capitalized, nationally recognized retail chains that are household names and patronized by the general public.

Triple Net Lease

Triple net lease means the tenant pays the rent and is also responsible for paying all the operating expenses relating to the property, including maintenance, taxes, and insurance. The financial stability of the tenant becomes an important risk factor.

All-Cash Deal

All cash means the investor acquires the property from the seller by paying 100 percent cash equal to the purchase price and does not enter into a mortgage. This strategy reduces the *leverage* (borrowing) associated with the transaction and could result in a greater portion of the rental income being taxed, since the interest expense associated with a mortgage isn't available to offset the income. The all-cash deals also contain a lot of idle equity that you might be able to put to better use elsewhere, depending on market conditions. Additionally, having all cash in the deal will effect a loss of the buying power of that cash, especially over a holding period of

10, 20, or even 30 years. This is the case even given some reasonable appreciation of the property owned.

> **leverage** the use of debt to purchase something more expensive than you could otherwise afford to buy for all cash. The most common form of leverage is the purchase of a home. For example, the house costs $250,000, but all you have in cash is $100,000. You accomplish the purchase with a mortgage of $150,000 leveraging your cash to acquire a $250,000 asset. The higher the degree of leverage, the greater the percentage of return on (or loss of) your money.

Low-Leverage Deal

The primary difference between an all-cash deal and a low-leverage deal is that in the latter some amount of cash is invested and the investor incurs a small mortgage or small financing package is put in place to cover the remainder of the purchase price. The smaller the amount of the mortgage package, the less leveraged the deal; the greater the amount of cash invested, the more like an all-cash deal it becomes.

Additional risks to real estate investments are vacancy and bankruptcy. There is no guarantee that the tenant will continue to occupy the property once the lease expires, and there is no guarantee that the landlord will collect the rent in the event the tenant goes bankrupt. These risks, along with the risk that the property will not appreciate as fast as other similar properties and the loss of buying power make it necessary for us to take these types of deals out of the low-risk category and include them here among the medium-risk group. Both real estate ownership and real estate investing have been touched on in several chapters of this book and are a complex subject.

CORPORATE BONDS (INVESTMENT-GRADE)

A corporate bond is really a mortgage, with you the bondholder acting as the bank/lender and the corporation as the borrower. Using our mythical ABC Company as the borrower and you as the lender, a typical corporate bond would look like the following:

✔ Face value: $10,000 (the amount you lent ABC Company).

✔ Maturity date: June 15, 2020 (on this date the company promises to repay the $10,000 borrowed).

✔ Interest: 6 percent payable every June 15 and December 15 (the semiannual or $300 fixed income you get for as long as you own the bond).

Typically, investors, brokers, and financial planners discuss bonds and other fixed-income securities in terms of *premium* and *discount*, with 100 representing 100 percent of the bond's face value. Perhaps you bought a bond at 96$\frac{1}{2}$ (96.5 percent of the face value) or $9,650. The difference of $350 between the $10,000 face value and the price you paid, $9,650, is known as a discount. You may have bought another bond at 102$\frac{1}{2}$ (102.5 percent of face value) or $10,250. In this case, you paid $250 over face value. This amount is known as a premium. In all cases the bond matures at 100 percent of face value or $10,000. Other bonds have a face value of $1,000.

premium　the difference between the face value/maturity value of a bond and its higher current market value. A bond selling at 104$\frac{1}{2}$ is selling at more than face value and is said to be at a premium of 4$\frac{1}{2}$ points. Also, the price of an option.

discount　purchase of a bond at an amount that is less than the face value or redemption value. A bond purchased at 95$\frac{3}{4}$ is bought at 95.75 percent of the face value or redemption value of $1000 or $957.50. Such a discounted purchase would mean the bondholder would receive a higher yield than if bought at face value.

Even if ABC Company was the greatest thing since sliced bread, there are a number of areas that would make such an investment riskier than low risk or no risk. The premium or discount may narrow or widen during the life of the bond (this may not be an issue in the event you intend to hold the bond until maturity). The credit quality of the issuer may change downward, over time, and this would have negative implications about the market value of your bond.

In 2020, when this bond matures, assuming the issuer repays the face value, the original $10,000 being returned will have lost considerable buying power to inflation. Over a multidecade period of time, that 6 percent interest rate you have been receiving buys fewer goods than before. The coupon may have looked attractive when you originally purchased the bond, but could be well below the prevailing interest rates in the next decade or two. And, clearly, ABC Company's future is yet another risk factor. Will it remain profitable? Can it stay competitive? Will it even still be in business? A look at the bond's rating (see munis section of this chapter for the various ratings) will help you decide whether the risk is worth taking. But, in any event, stick to those investment-grade ratings of AAA, AA, A, and BBB or Aaa, Aa, A, and Baa.

ZERO COUPON BONDS

Zero coupon bonds represent fixed-income securities that are issued at a discount to face value and do not pay interest during the life of the bond. At maturity, the issuer is obligated to pay the investor the face value of the bond. Perhaps the most common example of zero coupon bonds is U.S. Treasury bills that were discussed in Chapter 5.

> **zero coupon bonds**   bonds that pay no current coupon payments during their life, and are issued at a discount to face value or value at maturity.

Assuming the issuer is of a high credit quality, these securities face two major risks:

✔ The interest income on most of these securities is considered to be taxable in the year the interest accrues and is in the form of an accretion of the value of the security and not in the form of cash. This is also known as "shadow income." This means that the investor would owe income taxes on the interest income even though he or she receives no cash. For this reason, many investors position these securities in a tax-deferred account such as a retirement plan.

✔ Many of these securities have a long maturity. And, since the issuer makes no periodic interest payments, the security tends to be relatively volatile regarding changes in market interest rates. This factor can have a negative or positive effect if you want to sell the security prior to its maturity.

INCOME SECURITIES

A blue-chip stock, by definition, is the stock of a company that is considered to be mature and relatively stable. The theory is that a blue-chip company does well in good and bad economic times, is profitable on a consistent basis, and has a history of having paid out the major portion of its after-tax profits to its shareholders in the form of dividends. A typical blue chip might have a 50- to 75-year or longer history of never missing a quarterly dividend. The names of blue-chip companies will roll off the tip of your tongue: DuPont, Eastman Kodak, IBM, AT&T, Procter & Gamble, and Coca-Cola, to name a few.

An income security, usually a blue-chip common or preferred stock, is that of a company which has paid out those dividends over a very long period of time (in the form of cash dividends and/or *stock dividends*), is purchased for that income portion of your asset allocation model, and isn't necessarily held for the purposes of capital appreciation. That's not to say that income stocks don't also go up in value. These stocks have enjoyed and typically continue to enjoy appreciation as the market and the economy in general prosper. However—and this is one of the reasons we include income securities in the medium-risk category— the payment of dividends is at the whim of the board of directors of the company and dividends can be reduced or skipped altogether depending on the company's changing fortunes and financial strength. Also, the key to the income retaining its purchasing power is that the company increases its dividend over time.

> **stock dividends** dividends paid to shareholders in the form of additional shares of the company's stock rather than in cash. During its growth phase a company would want to conserve cash and use it to continue to expand. By paying dividends in the form of shares instead of cash, it can accomplish both goals.

S&P 500 INDEX MUTUAL FUNDS

Today, *index* investing has become increasingly popular. Since so many individuals participate in mutual funds that invest in a broad index of securities such as a bond index, the S&P 500 Index of common stocks, the

Russell 2000 index, and the Wilshire 5000 index, we thought that it was important to discuss these types of investments. Many people think that an investment in the S&P 500 Index is a relatively low-risk investment. People draw this conclusion for two reasons: the U.S. stock market has soared since 1982, and only approximately 15 percent of all mutual funds beat the S&P 500 Index on a regular basis.

> **index**   a measurement of change. The Dow Jones Industrial Average measures the fluctuation of the 30 components that make up that index. There are indexes for the New York Stock Exchange, the American Stock Exchange, the Standard & Poor's 500, and the Value Line, just to name a few.

Here are a few risks associated with indexes and index funds that you should consider, especially when establishing your asset allocation:

✔ Any index consists of the individual securities that comprise the index. In other words, the value of your index mutual fund is determined by the value of the individual securities that make up that index. If the stock market falls, the value of your S&P Index mutual fund should fall as well.

✔ An index still bears risk based on the market that it is invested in. Don't conclude that since you are investing in a well-diversified index that you are immune from market dips. Most index funds tend to maintain their investment weightings regardless of the market itself. Rather, they trade based on investment inflows and outflows and changes to the members of the index. This has been effective, especially in a rising stock market. But in the event of a bear market, the index should fall at least as much as the market.

✔ Often an index is overpowered by one segment of securities. In the case of the S&P 500, the value of the index is largely determined by the value of *large-cap (large-capitalization) stock* such as General Electric, Coca-Cola, Intel, and Microsoft. Essentially, this is largely a blue chip fund.

large-cap (large-capitalization) stock   stock of a company where the market value of all of its common stock that is issued and outstanding exceeds $5 billion (this number is a market convention and may change over time).

FOREIGN COMMON STOCKS (BLUE CHIPS)

Today, many investors appropriately diversify their holdings by investing a portion of their portfolio in foreign stocks or mutual funds that invest in common stocks of foreign companies. Examples include purchasing shares of Hong Kong Telecommunications, the major telephone company based in Hong Kong, or purchasing shares of Cadbury Schweppes, a consumer goods company based in London. Mutual funds typically buy shares of overseas companies directly on the local stock exchange of the foreign country or by acquiring American depositary receipts (ADRs) or American depositary shares (ADSs). ADRs represent shares of the company's common stock held in trust for the benefit of the investor.

Typically, these foreign companies experience different growth rates and face economic forces that differ from the factors facing U.S. companies. For these reasons, the common stocks of foreign companies have had a relatively low correlation with U.S. common stocks. However, over time as globalization continues, it is likely that foreign and U.S. domestic common stocks will be more highly correlated and will be more likely to move in the same direction.

With foreign companies, there are additional risks, including:

✔ Political risk (the stability of the government).

✔ Currency risk (foreign exchange limits and concerns).

✔ Economic risk (the volatility of the local economy).

These foreign blue chips can be a favorable way to allocate your assets and achieve the diversification you are seeking. Due to the risks and issues we discussed above, we place foreign blue chips in the medium risk category.

FOREIGN BONDS

Foreign bonds are fixed-income securities issued by governments of foreign countries and by companies based in countries outside the United States. The investment theory is that by purchasing fixed-income securities from a wide variety of issuers around the globe, investors can diversify their portfolio and achieve a higher yield while assuming the same or relatively lower risk. One concern with foreign bonds is that the issuers (debtors) typically pay the interest income in local currency; then those units of local currency are converted into U.S. dollars. Assuming the issuer is based in the United Kingdom and pays the coupon in pounds sterling, when the U.S. dollar weakens, that fixed coupon denominated in pounds sterling converts into more U.S. dollars and buys additional goods. And the opposite is true as well. Also, foreign debt securities are subject to a sovereign ceiling. This means that any company based in a particular country will not achieve a credit rating that exceeds the country's credit rating.

foreign bonds   fixed-income securities issued by governments of foreign countries and by companies based in countries outside the United States.

We place foreign bonds in the medium-risk category but at the riskier end of the spectrum.

There are several ways to profit from holding fixed-income securities. One way is to purchase the security at a discount to its face value and hold the bond to maturity, when the issuer redeems it at face value. The most common way to earn income from fixed-income securities is from the periodic coupon. The other way is to buy the fixed-income securities of an issuer with a relatively poor but improving credit rating. As the issuer's credit rating improves, the bond should appreciate in value. For these reasons and the relatively speculative nature and lower stability of foreign bonds, we consider these types of investments to be relatively risky.

PREFERRED STOCKS

Preferred stocks, on the other hand, offer a little more of a comfort level as it applies to dividends (your income from that class of security) since the preferred stockholder's dividend must be paid before a common dividend can be paid, and many preferred stocks have a number of features that make that receipt of dividends even more secure:

✔ *Preferred.* Not only must the preferred dividend be paid before the common dividend, but also the preferred stockholder comes before the common stockholder in the liquidation of the company, should that happen.

✔ *Convertible.* Some classes of preferred stock are also *convertible* into common shares of the same corporation. That convertible feature gives the shareholder additional choices. If the convertible preferred shares are worth more than the common shares into which they are convertible, you keep the convertible preferred. If, on the other hand, the common shares are worth more, you convert the preferred into common stock and sell the common stock or hold it with the objective of capturing future appreciation.

convertible a security that can be changed into another security—for example, a convertible bond or convertible preferred stock that can be exchanged for shares of the company's common stock.

✔ *Cumulative.* Some classes of convertible preferred stocks may be also cumulative. This has the effect of protecting you against the board of directors who might have voted to skip the dividends in a period or periods altogether. In this case the *cumulative preferred* stockholders are owed all the skipped dividends and must have all the arrears made up before another common dividend can be paid.

cumulative preferred a share of preferred stock where the company must pay all dividends due on preferred stock before declaring any dividends to the common stockholders and owes you the arrears.

✔ *Fixed-dollar dividend/percent dividend.* Certain classes of preferred stocks pay a fixed dollar or $4.75 cumulative preferred and some issues base their dividends on a percentage or 4.75 percent cumulative preferred. It is important to determine what the percentage dividend is based on. For example, many preferred stocks pay dividends as a percentage of the preferred stock's par value. In this case, the par value is unlikely to change, so this is effectively a fixed-dollar dividend. With other issues, the dividend may fluctuate based on an index. For planning purposes the predictability of the fixed-dollar preferred seems to make more sense.

✔ *Callable.* Some preferred stock issues can be called or redeemed by the issuer. Sometimes these issues can be called by the company at a price fixed in advance. Generally, the redemption or call price rises over time. This feature enables the company to retire the preferred stock prior to its maturity. This is particularly powerful regarding convertible preferred. If the company redeems the convertible preferred stock before the holders can convert the preferred into common stock, the company avoids *dilution* to earnings per share that a conversion would cause. The call price and its relationship to the current market, coupled with the conversion feature, can give rise to some interesting trading possibilities that are usually taken advantage of by a professional known as an arbitrageur.

> **dilution**   literally, "watering down" the value of shares by a subsequent recapitalization of a company. Example of dilution of ownership: You own 100 shares of a company with 1000 shares issued and outstanding. At this point you hold 10 percent of the shares. The company issues and sells another 1000 shares to the general public. Now you own 100 out of 2000 shares, or 5 percent.

For maximum safety as well as the maximum number of choices, you might want to ask your securities professional to look around for a callable, convertible, cumulative preferred stock that pays a quarterly or semiannual fixed-dollar dividend. Typically, the dividend on a convertible is less than the dividend on a nonconvertible.

We just mentioned only a few of the blue chip companies that you can consider for this category of your asset allocation model. The choice of high-quality companies is quite broad. The 30 companies in the Dow Jones Industrial Average, the S&P 500 companies, and a number of public utilities may fit the medium-risk asset portfolio.

EQUIPMENT LEASING TRANSACTIONS (INCOME DEALS)

Equipment leasing transactions are similar to real estate rental property in that an owner buys something and rents it to a user. These transactions are usually in the form of a limited partnership. Equipment found in such transactions would be used by the trucking industry, airlines, and the railroads as well as the computer market. The partnership collects rental income from the lessee, uses the cash flow to service any debt, and then distributes any free cash to the partners. The income can be partially tax-free due to the use of depreciation within the partnership. Depreciation deductions arise from the periodic write-off of the equipment over the lease term. At the end of the lease, the partnership attempts either to lease the equipment again or to sell it off (disposal).

> **equipment leasing transactions**   similar to real estate rental property; an owner buys equipment and rents it to a user.

The risk factors attached to this group would include:

✔ Whether the entity leasing the equipment can continue to make the lease payments (credit quality).

✔ If, at the end of the lease, the partnership can release the equipment again to the same or another lessee.

✔ If, at the end of the lease, there is a resale market for the equipment. Remember, if the equipment is computers, they become obsolete relatively quickly. Investors can reduce this risk by assuming a lower residual (value of the equipment at lease end); this results in higher rental payments during the lease term.

✔ Whether the transaction makes sense on its own economic merits. The Tax Reform Act of 1986 largely eliminated passive losses so most individuals lost their ability to use depreciation deductions to offset their other income. The leasing market is dominated by institutional investors such as major finance companies, banks, financial institutions, and the credit companies of major industrial corporations. As a result, it is extremely important that you analyze the value of any leased property carefully.

You must consider all these risks. We rate leasing deals to be of medium risk in spite of the fact that the equipment in question might even have been leased to the federal government.

OIL AND GAS (INCOME PROGRAMS)

Oil and gas programs comprise another category of deal that is structured inside a limited partnership, but in this case for the following purposes:

✔ Purchase existing wells already producing gas.
✔ Purchase existing wells already producing oil.
✔ Drill new wells seeking gas reserves.
✔ Drill new wells seeking oil reserves.

Although the profits from such activities can be beyond belief if a significant discovery is made in any of the drilling programs, there is also the distinct possibility that nothing will be found and your dollars would be at significant risk. A similar risk applies to the purchase of an existing well, in the sense that it may be a gusher today, but may not be a gusher tomorrow, next week, or next year. By engaging in this type of program, you, the investor, may receive significant write-offs during the first year of a drilling program or engage in a strictly income-producing program that is pumping oil out of existing wells and selling it into the market. Part of the payment you receive from such programs is also from depletion allowances and depreciation. Your personal tax adviser must be consulted to fit such programs into your asset mix.

Obviously, if the price of oil and the price of gas fall in the global markets, you stand to suffer considerable losses. We consider these to be at the higher end of the medium risk category. However, if you can utilize the tax deductions from a drilling project and you participate in wells that are already proven, you can hedge your risk to some extent.

DERIVATIVE SECURITIES

Already discussed in detail as Low-risk investments at the end of Chapter 5, DIAMONDS and spiders, two derivative securities, were being used to hedge your portfolio. Clearly, if you hedge a low-risk portfolio, you must hedge all portfolios.

The way we suggested to use DIAMONDS and spiders to hedge that low-risk portfolio would be repeated here and we would add some additional types of securities to hedge that bond portfolio, portfolio of income securities, and even your investment property. By entering the futures arena and employing some of the interest rate futures, index futures, currency futures, and energy futures it is possible to put a hedge around your debt securities, mortgages, oil and gas deals, and virtually every other investment category used. Since the world of futures represents a $200,000,000,000,000+ ($200 trillion) marketplace and takes place around the clock, around the globe in virtually every currency, it's really the topic of another book. It is suggested that you engage someone from the futures arena (check that professional out carefully) to position such hedges for you.

STARTING YOUR OWN BUSINESS

Today, more and more individuals are starting their own businesses. Typically, this endeavor is relatively risky. Often, observers think of starting a business or other entrepreneurial venture as a major wholehearted, bet-your-life endeavor. This does not have to be the case. Many people start a business on a step-by-step basis, invest small amounts over time, and build their business in a sequential fashion. Sometimes they start their business as an outgrowth of their hobby or they provide a service based on a specific skill they have. This strategy tends to reduce the risk related to starting a business.

We are placing starting your own business in the medium-risk category based on achieving most or all of the following assumptions:

✔ The founder has a specific niche, skill, or expertise—specialized knowledge in the subject matter or a differential advantage. One example is an accountant who works in a company or an accounting firm, gets experience, and starts his or her own accounting firm.

✔ The business concept is a proven idea or the founder can demonstrate that there is a high likelihood that the business will be successful.

✔ The founder has demonstrated success or clear traits as an entrepreneur.

✔ The founder's initial investment in the business is relatively small (compared to the founder's net worth).

✔ The business is headquartered at home where the incremental fixed costs of operating the business are minimal.

✔ The business is a service business or a type of business where the founder can collect revenue before spending significant amounts on equipment or raw materials.

✔ The founder has income from another job or from another source such as a spouse or partner.

✔ The founder makes a complete and thorough business plan and conducts market research.

FRANCHISING

Today, franchising is a popular way to get into business. Franchising means buying into a company and purchasing a store or the right to sell a product or product line in a specific geographic territory. In some ways, franchising is similar to buying a job. To become a franchisee, the investor has to pay an up-front fee (some franchisors offer financing). In addition, the franchisee is required to pay ongoing fees that are either a percentage of sales revenue or a requirement to purchase a certain amount of supplies and products from the franchisor company.

Some franchises such as McDonald's, Dunkin' Donuts, and Burger King are established programs. In some ways, there is lower risk associated with becoming a franchisee with these companies. With the more established programs, the initiation fees are higher. With less established and more speculative franchises, the initiation fees are typically lower, but there is greater risk that the franchise program will fail.

If you are considering becoming a franchisee, it is important to conduct thorough research on the franchisor company and the viability of the concept. Without exception, you should hire a lawyer, and perhaps you should also hire a business adviser to help protect your rights and your investment.

Chapter

High-Risk Assets

I n the previous two chapters, we discussed the fact that low-risk assets would comprise a relatively small percentage of most people's
portfolios and medium-risk assets would comprise a relatively large
percentage. This leaves high-risk assets, which represent the most
volatile and least certain asset class. Most people should allocate no
more than 10 percent to 15 percent of their portfolio to the high-risk asset category.

HIGH-RISK ASSET CATEGORY EXPLAINED

High-risk assets are investments that are relatively unstable. The market
value tends to fluctuate widely and there is a relatively high probability
that you will lose some or all of your money.

RISKS WITH HIGH-RISK ASSETS

The two main risks with high-risk assets are high volatility and loss of investment. High volatility means that the fair market value of the investment at a given point in time is difficult to predict. One example of this is
a small-cap common stock that experiences wide price fluctuations. Loss
of investment means that you lose your money.

Another important consideration with high-risk assets is liquidity;
how quickly can you sell the asset to raise cash? You cannot easily sell a
high-risk asset to raise cash. Either the selling process takes a relatively

long period of time or the selling costs such as the bid and ask spread, transfer taxes and fees, or the sales commission are relatively high.

PLACE IN PORTFOLIO

High-risk assets serve several purposes in a portfolio. First, they can be exciting and thrilling. Sometimes, a high-risk asset can turn out to increase in value 10 or more times your initial investment. In other words, a success can yield riches.

As you read this book, you will learn that the model portfolios or percentages we discuss are suggested numbers and allocations only. Your personal risk tolerance levels for each category discussed may be more or less than those suggested percentages; you should establish a plan that meets your goals and objectives. It is perfectly acceptable for a 40-year-old to be at more than 60 percent risk if that level is understood, the investments used are understood, and you are prepared to lose money. This does not necessarily mean that you *will* lose money, but the more risky the asset class, the more likely you are to incur losses. The same would apply to an 80-year-old who simply has enough wealth and wants to play the market with 50 percent of his or her assets. Again, the final answer must come from you as to what's good for you, understood by you, and can be tolerated by you.

All of the following examples of high-risk assets can be combined or used individually to create the asset allocation model that fits your asset allocation requirements. You may decide to spread your portfolio proportionally among all of the following or split it between two groups. Or, perhaps you will elect to avoid this category altogether.

STARTING YOUR OWN BUSINESS

Starting a business in this case differs from the scenario discussed in Chapter 6, because the business is riskier or the circumstances are riskier, as follows:

✔ The business concept is new and unproven.
✔ The founder has no particular expertise or proven track record.
✔ The investment represents a relatively large percentage of the founder's net worth.

✔ The business is more speculative or is a fad.

✔ The founder has little or no other sources of income to fall back on if the venture fails.

SPECULATIVE FRANCHISES

In Chapter 6, we discussed franchises and becoming a franchisee. We place speculative franchises in the high-risk asset category because they entail the investor assuming more risk. Perhaps the franchise concept is unproven; the franchise is a new business idea and has not been thoroughly tested. Another risk might be that your territory, the area in which you are licensed to operate, is poorly defined or can be changed by the franchisor at will. Perhaps the up-front and ongoing investments are relatively high in relation to the expected return on investment. With these franchises, it may be possible to hit the jackpot and become wealthy. However, it is also highly likely that you will lose all of your money. Get sound, expert business advice, study the franchise concept, and write a complete business plan and market study before you invest your money.

RARE COINS

The small change in your pocket or pocketbook could very well be worth just small change, or perhaps be worth many times the face value of the coins. It is difficult to discern the difference between pocket change and true rare coins (*numismatic* coins).

numismatic relating to the study of or collection of coins. As opposed to intrinsic value (the value of the metal in said coin), a coin's numismatic value would be based on its population (how many were ever produced), its historic significance, and its condition.

Before considering rare coins, it is necessary for you to establish a relationship with a coin dealer or other rare coin expert who is known in your community, certified and registered, and a member of one or more of the nationally recognized coin dealer associations. Most of us, the authors included, wouldn't know one grade level from another, the *population* (just how many of that particular coin exist today and in what condition) of the coins in question, or the historical significance of one coin versus another. Specialized knowledge, advice, and expertise are the key. Buy only the best issues you can afford, the highest quality, and the smallest population to ensure better marketability.

> **population**   in the world of coins and stamps, the number of a particular item that were at one time minted or printed. Pennies have been minted in the United States by the billions every year and have a huge population/low value. Postage stamps are usually printed by the hundred million. A stamp or coin with a low population would generally bespeak greater value. Silver coins whose populations have been reduced by being melted down for their intrinsic value when silver ran up above $40 per ounce are now worth more than before.

Coins are a hard asset and their value, subject to the above considerations, will generally move with interest rates and inflation. Coins by themselves do not generate periodic cash income. Typically, hard assets become more valuable as interest rates trend higher and during periods of rising inflation, and drop in value when those barometers reverse direction. The following factors lead to increased values of your coin collection:

✔ The rarer the coin.
✔ The smaller the population.
✔ The higher the grade (uncirculated or proof).
✔ The greater the historical significance.

Know what you're doing, work with a recognized expert, and invest in rare coins with your eyes open.

The exception to all of the above would be investment in *bullion* coins instead of the numismatic coins just described. Bullion coins have a value directly related to the value of the metal content of each coin rather than the coin's population, condition, or historic significance. A one-ounce gold or silver coin, in virtually any condition, will be worth that day's value of the metal itself (minus a sales commission).

> **bullion**   the actual gold, silver, or platinum metal, typically in bar form, traded based on the actual value of the metal without numismatic considerations. Bullion coins are traded based on the value of the metal irrespective of collectible considerations or history.

Additional risk factors when investing in rare coins would include their storage and safekeeping and those costs, as well as the cost to insure them. Another factor to consider is the high cost involved in buying and selling coins. The bid and ask spreads (markup) tend to be relatively high, and sales commissions can equal 3 percent to 5 percent of the value of the coins.

PRECIOUS GEMS

Once again we are looking at a relatively high-risk investment that re-quires/demands expertise and specialized knowledge. If you were shown a 10-carat diamond in one hand and a 10-carat zircon in the other, both equally cut and set, could you tell that one might be worth $80,000 and the other $8,000? In reality, neither can many jewelers!—sometimes not even the jeweler down the block who fixed your watch and sold you those nice bracelets. The answer is to consult a recognized, registered, and certi-fied gemologist.

The value of precious gems is subject to quality, size, color, cut, clar-ity, and facets. As with rare coins, the population of that particular quality, interest rates, and inflation all affect value, and the gems must be stored and properly insured against loss.

PRECIOUS METALS

Since most investors participate in the futures market when it comes to precious metals, rather than owning the actual metals themselves, let's first look there.

Statistically, over 90 percent of those people who participate in the world of futures lose money. The other 10 percent make out like bandits. In other words, the money lost by the 90 percent plus is made by the less than 10 percent who profit. This is why you hear about killings being made in this marketplace. Yes, some people do make money, but most don't. The futures market is a zero-sum game. This means that the winners' profits equal the others' losses. Considering that the futures markets comprise the biggest marketplace in the world (over $200 trillion is traded annually around the clock, around the globe), all of those risks come together in your trades.

The international currency risks, global government unrest and lack of stability, the entire international interest rate arena, and the weather in each part of the world represented all come to bear on virtually every trade. Perhaps you buy silver mined in one country and that country's currency moves against the dollar; you could lose before the trade settles. Political unrest in a gold mining country causes the mines to close down and the gold supply from that country to dry up. Other countries dump supply on the market and the stability of that market disappears. The risks of trading in the futures arena are so great that this type of trading will be discussed in greater detail later in this chapter. Perhaps the most significant risk investors face in the futures market is leverage. A small investment controls a relatively large position in the underlying asset. As a result, small movements in the price of the underlying asset can result in large moves in the value of the futures contracts.

Ownership of the actual metals themselves brings along the risk of storage and insurance, the dilution suffered if you have to liquidate just a small portion of your holdings and have the remainder reconfigured into new bars or coins, and the fact that not everyone wants to buy raw metals—many would rather have bullion coins. These are the risk factors you, the owner of the raw metals, have to face.

Investing in metals, regardless of the way you do so (coins, bars, futures, shares of mining companies, etc.) again requires you to understand the language and the nature of the metals.

HIGHLY LEVERAGED REAL ESTATE, REAL ESTATE DEVELOPMENT, RAW LAND

Real Estate

In Chapter 6 we discussed leveraged real estate in the sense that a property owned with debt financing places the owner at risk that the property might not keep up with inflation and might not be able to be rented at a profitable rate or occupancy level. Think of how much more risk you face if the property is highly leveraged and maybe carries 80 percent debt financing. The higher financing means that there is less room for you to have a vacancy for any period of time because you have to make those mortgage payments regardless of whether tenants occupy the property. With little or no equity in a highly leveraged deal, there is no room for you to borrow against the equity for necessary repairs or improvements or even to buy additional properties. If interest rates become more favorable (go down) while that property hasn't gone up in value keeping pace with the market, and you haven't been able to pay down that huge mortgage, you won't be able to refinance to take advantage of those lower rates. To refinance, you would probably have to put up additional equity capital to pay down the old mortgage and provide personal guarantees and perhaps additional collateral.

Real Estate Development

The simple problem here is that you are building a house and bearing all of the risk of investment. Under a planned project, you might invest some of the money to acquire the land and perhaps build some of the infrastructure (roads, sewers, etc.). Before you break ground and begin building a structure, you sell the home. This strategy means you sign a contract where the buyer agrees to pay you if you meet certain milestones. The key question is, if I build a spec house, can I sell it? Many developers have acquired a beautiful tract of land, maybe even with a waterfront view, started to build a nice development, and found it difficult or impossible to sell off the houses built. Maybe the community turned out to be overbuilt; that planned nearby mall or schools or other facilities never got developed; the town became so overpopulated that tax rates rose way above expectations making the new houses simply unaffordable; or during development interest rates rose to such levels that the average buyer couldn't afford the payments and simply didn't buy. An interesting exception is the development of very expensive (multimillion-dollar) homes that come fully decorated, fully furnished, some even with a car or two in the garage, and all you have to do is move in and unpack your clothing. Of course, the average homeowner doesn't spend $3 million or more for a home, but more likely just a few hundred thousand dollars.

Raw Land

Raw land is a vacant tract of property. The classic statement about raw land is, "Raw land consumes cash and yields nothing." Depending on the location and the circumstances, investors have made fortunes by investing in raw land. One example is land in the Silicon Valley area of California, home to many high-technology companies. Early investors sold out to real estate developers who built headquarters and factories and other structures that housed these high-tech giants.

- ✔ Investors buy raw land for appreciation, development, or farming.
- ✔ Until the land is utilized, the land generates no cash return.
- ✔ Some investors convert raw land into a farming property or a parking lot. This enables the owner to generate some sort of cash returns.
- ✔ During the holding period, the investor still has to pay the mortgage and loses the opportunity cost on that idle equity.
- ✔ Whatever the value of the property and no matter where it's located, raw land requires property tax payments.
- ✔ Raw land (and developed property) may be subject to certain legal and regulatory issues such as zoning, environmental, and use rules.

Given the above factors as well as the fact that the raw land has only a few uses (depending on its location), we place raw land into this high-risk category.

If you own real property, you might consider a 1031 like-kind tax-free exchange. This entails working with a third-party intermediary and swapping your property for another property. If this transaction is executed properly, it typically defers your paying capital gains tax on the property you transfer to the third party.

This will enable you to trade the equity in your land for a similar amount of equity in another piece of investment property and channel your money into the new investment. This technique is very much like trading baseball cards.

LEVERAGED EQUIPMENT LEASING

In Chapter 6 we discussed equipment leasing deals from the standpoint of income, and placed such transactions into the medium-risk group. If such deals aren't structured for income and perhaps are also very highly leveraged (the deal is loaded with debt financing) we have to put such deals into the high-risk category. With leveraged leasing transactions, we face the same risk factors discussed in Chapter 6, but must also add the uncertainty of being able to cover all of that debt financing as well as the uncertain future of interest rates, coupled with the credit strength of the lessee and the uncertainty of leasing or selling the property at lease end.

INDIVIDUAL COMMON STOCKS

In Chapters 5 and 6, we noted that individual stocks could be in the low-risk group and also in the medium-risk group, depending on the risk factors discussed. We must also include individual stocks in the high-risk group for the following reasons:

- ✔ Buying a single stock or issue means you forfeit the diversification that a mutual fund offers.
- ✔ The company may be a start-up business with little or no financial track record, history, sales, or even profits.
- ✔ Shares of the company's stock may be what we call penny stocks (stocks selling at under $5 per share) and traded in the relatively volatile NASDAQ marketplace or on foreign exchanges or in foreign currencies. The management of the company may be novices who are in their first business venture.
- ✔ The company may be poorly capitalized and unable to borrow working capital or raise other dollars to fund expansion, distribution, and marketing.
- ✔ The market price of the company's stock might be quite high due to speculation; that is, it is selling at a multiple of earnings way above the market's norm (see Chapter 2 as it applies to P/E ratios).
- ✔ The stock of the company may have just been downgraded from "buy" to "hold" or even "sell" by a major brokerage firm analyst.
- ✔ The products of the company may not be as competitive as they once were or are simply becoming unpopular, obsolete, or outdated.
- ✔ The company may be a one-product/one-service company and all your eggs would be in just that basket and not balanced by a conglomerate that offers multiple products for sale.
- ✔ There may be such a small float (number of shares held by the public) that if you wanted to liquidate some of your holdings,

your sale would adversely move the market and reduce the value of your remaining stock.

✔ The company may execute a merger or takeover that could result in diluting the value of your investment.

After you have reread the risks in Chapters 5 and 6 and reviewed the above risks as they apply to individual stocks, you may want to reallocate your individual stock portfolio or simply move those already allocated assets into mutual funds with the same investment objectives. (See Chapter 8 for a more detailed discussion on mutual funds and their place in your portfolio.)

Individual Small-Cap Common Stocks

Small-cap stocks are common stocks of relatively small companies. These companies tend to be relatively young—in other words, start-ups. They also tend to be more volatile and often followed by fewer brokerage house analysts. It is important that you research these investments very carefully before investing your money. These investments should be considered part of the high-risk asset category.

Individual Foreign Small-Cap Common Stocks

Foreign small-cap common stocks carry the same risks as small-cap common stocks and foreign stocks. These stocks require particularly thorough research.

OPTIONS (FOR SPECULATION)

Options are rights to purchase common stock from (call options) or sell common stock to (put options) the writer of the option at a specified price within a specified time period. In Chapters 5 and 6 we discussed options in the form of covered calls and purchasing puts to hedge our portfolios. Those options strategies were designed to reduce the volatility of one's portfolio and create extra current income for the writer of a covered call option. Here we discuss another kind of option, stock options, as a speculative tool.

Corporations issue *stock options* to management and other key employees as an incentive to join the company or as a reward for specific performance. Companies grant stock options that vest over a period of years and entitle the holder (employee) the right to purchase shares of the company stock at a specific strike price at a specific point in time. These options are particularly popular in start-up companies and high-technology companies. Certainly, many stock options are held for a period of time during which the price of the underlying stock goes up and the holder of such options exercises those options at the lower exercise price and sells the stock at a gain. But, success stories about a stock price rising so the value of the stock option increased 10 times are the minority rather than the norm.

stock option not to be confused with a put or call option, a stock option is usually issued to valued employees, allowing them to purchase shares of the company's stock at a predetermined price for a number of years into the future. Hopefully, when those options are exercised and the shares are purchased their market value at that time will be considerably higher than the exercise price.

Such stories are speculation. The purchaser of the option was making a bet, similar to placing a bet at a casino. In the earlier chapters, we discussed using options as a hedge to protect your portfolio or produce extra current income. In this example, the investor is paying premiums (plus commissions) to buy put options or call options. This means the buyer of the options expects the price of the stock to move in a particular direction within a particular period of time.

For example, suppose the investor purchases an Intel Corporation January 90 call for a premium of $7. Listed options control 100 shares of common stock. So, the option buyer paid $700 ($7 per share multiplied by 100 shares) plus the commission. This option gives the buyer the right to purchase 100 shares of Intel Corporation common stock for $90 per share between the day he or she buys the option and the day it expires in January. Options derive their value based on a number of factors including volatility of the underlying common stock, the time until expiration, and the relationship of the strike price ($90 in this example) compared to the market value of the stock.

In this example, let's assume that Intel common stock trades at $80 per share. This option would be considered out-of-the-money since the option strike price equals $90 per share. The $7 premium represents the time value of the option. In other words, the option or right has value between now and the day the option expires in January. As we approach January, there is less time or life remaining for the option. At the expiration date, the option dies.

On the expiration date, the key to the option's value is the market value of the stock. If Intel common stock trades at $90 or less, the option is worthless. If the Intel common stock trades at a price between $90 and $97, the buyer of the option has lost money. This loss arises from the fact that the buyer paid a $7 premium to buy the option. If Intel common stock trades higher than $97, the option buyer has made a profit.

The tricky part about options in this example is that the buyer has to be correct on two points: the price of the underlying common stock and the time period. If the price of Intel common stock jumps to $100 in February, this is too late. The January $90 call option already expired.

Think of the following points concerning speculating in incentive stock options:

✔ If the person who was originally granted that stock option is now selling it, you have to ask yourself why. Remember that the original holder of the stock option was most likely a part of the management of the company and certainly knows more about the company than you possibly could. The other groups of people who sell options are investors who want to sell covered call premiums to generate extra current cash income. Either they think that the stock price will not rise above the option strike price or they are content to sell the stock at the strike price and retain the option premium.

✔ The original holders of stock options cannot use the excuse that they didn't have the cash to exercise their own stock options. If such stock options were worth something, there are plenty of lenders who'll lend money for the express purpose of allowing the holder to exercise their options and expect to be repaid from the profits realized from exercising the option and selling the stock.

✔ Are you, the new owner of that option, able to accept the risk of the stock's price declining right after you purchase the call option? Remember that a stock option is very much like a call in that you freeze the purchase price of the underlying stock and make your profit if the stock rises above the strike price, when you exercise the option, purchase the stock, and then sell the stock into the market.

✔ Are you, the new owner of that option, able to accept the risk of not being able to resell the option itself should the market price of the underlying stock not move in your favor? You can more easily resell a put or call option because they are, in most cases, traded on recognized exchanges, but incentive stock options aren't as readily marketable.

FUTURES

The subject of another book or two, *futures* (the trading in commodities including grains, orange juice, metals, and meats as well as interest rate futures) is an arena that you should become more knowledgeable about before you execute any futures trades.

> **futures** the trading in commodities such as grains, orange juice, metals, and even interest rates.

The world of futures involves trading activity in other than stocks and bonds that is going on around the world, in every country, in virtually every currency, around the clock and in dollar amounts, globally, that exceed the combined trading activity on most of the world's exchanges. Trading in the futures arena is estimated to exceed $200 trillion per year. This is perhaps the most volatile marketplace in existence today. Volatility is one of the biggest risk factors futures traders face. This should not overshadow the other factors inherent in a specific commodity such as global currency values, global government stability, the weather, and a whole host of other risks.

Remembering that over 90 percent of the people who trade futures lose money, you should only use 100 percent risk capital for this category. If what you have bet on happening in the future (that crop, energy demand, orange juice consumption, orange production, etc.) doesn't happen or happens to a lesser extent than anticipated, you stand to lose some or all of your dollars. On the other hand, using futures as a hedge (see Chapter 5) removes a large percentage of the risk and, if used properly, can actually offset downside risk entirely.

It is suggested that you allocate that very small percentage of your risk capital, or, maybe none of your capital, to speculating in the futures markets. If you decide to play this market, work with your financial professional's input to create proper hedges in the futures market around all positions possible.

OIL AND GAS DRILLING, EXPLORATION, AND MINING

The risks attached to oil and gas programs were discussed in Chapter 6 as they applied to income-oriented transactions and referenced regarding drilling and exploration. It is appropriate to reiterate a few of the points discussed earlier, since drilling, exploration and mining programs have a certain attractiveness and appeal. Investors find these types of investments to be exciting. Many people have made significant money in these deals, but most investors have lost fortunes. Don't think that you'll become another wealthy oil tycoon just by putting a few dollars into an oil drilling or exploration program.

Whether the deal involves drilling for oil or natural gas, there is relatively high risk of not finding any natural resources or discovering a minute quantity that is uneconomical to take out of the ground. Some of these drilling programs offer certain income tax advantages (investors are allowed to deduct "intangible drilling costs" against their other income), but unless you can take advantage of these deductions in the years they are available to you and in the amounts credited, they are wasted. Contact your tax professional to make a determination about the value of these deductions and credits to you. Even if these deductions and credits are available to you, you are still likely to lose your entire investment if the drilling program fails.

Exploring for either oil or gas reserves entails the same risk factors discussed for drilling programs, with perhaps fewer dollars at risk per deal. Mining, on the other hand, may be even riskier than drilling, since the costs are greater in many cases and mining involves more environmental considerations. If you drill for oil or gas on the ocean floor, you aren't disturbing fields or forests and don't have to replace whole farms that might have been disturbed in the process. A great deal of surface mining (as opposed to in the ground holes dug for whatever mineral is being sought) involves digging up acres of open land that not only becomes visually unattractive as a result of the digging, but also compromises the crops and animals that would otherwise grow on the surface. These added restoration costs in addition to the actual digging or exploration costs, if nothing else, make mining all the more risky.

Since the resale value of the oil, gas, or materials mined depends on spot market prices and the global futures markets as well as the global currency and interest rate markets, even if these programs are successful, the mined minerals may not be worth the cost of mining them.

COMMODITIES

Commodities are physical assets such as grain, food, minerals, precious metals, and natural resources. Three of the major categories of economic value involving commodities are *actuals*, futures, and indexes.

> **commodities** the physical assets including meats, orange juice, and metals, including gold and silver.

> **actuals** trading in the commodity itself; at the end of the life of a futures contract, the owner actually receives or takes delivery of the gold, silver, soybeans, and so on.

1. *Actuals.* The actual physical commodity in the form of pork bellies, soybeans, gold, silver, and so on.

2. *Futures.* Trading positions to take delivery of or sell the physical commodity at some point in time in the future at a specified price today. Futures are executed through contracts. In practice, investors typically don't take delivery of the commodity; rather, they settle their positions in cash.

3. *Indexes.* Trading in neither the actual nor the future, but a derivative-like security representing the various commodities indexes watched by all commodities traders.

We must consider commodities trading to be another asset category where we place 100 percent of our money at risk. If we play in this arena, we must be prepared to lose 100 percent or even more, depending on our leverage, of our investment.

It is important to consider other associated risk factors that would involve the particular commodity. The value of any of the precious metals (gold, silver, platinum, copper, etc.) would be subject to interest rates and the condition of the global economy at large. It is important to consider the impact of any governments trying either to buy or to sell the commodity in large quantities. One example is the recent sale of a number of governments' gold reserves. Components of the energy index (crude oil, natural gas, unleaded gasoline, heating oil, etc.) would be subject to seasonal demand by the public, supplies available in strategic stockpiles around the globe, and the reserves in the ground. Corn, wheat, barley, oats, soybeans, and so on (the components of the grain segment) would react to changing weather conditions in the growing regions, consumption by the public around the globe, governmental purchases for the purposes of price control, and a host of other variables. The soft or miscellaneous commodities like orange juice, cotton, coffee, cocoa, and sugar each carry their own risks stemming from demand, supply, weather, and political and economic conditions, to mention just a few. We should also include the meat group (hogs, cattle, pork bellies, etc.) as another group affected by supply, the weather, the economies of the buying countries, and so on in an effort to give as complete a picture of the risks as possible.

MOVIE INVESTMENTS

Movies are particularly glamorous and alluring. People become engrossed with seeing their names in lights as well as rubbing elbows with the stars. Investing in films can be very exciting. In 1997, the film *Titanic* became the first movie in the history of the motion picture industry to gross over $1,000,000,000 (yes, one billion dollars). With all the media play and publicity, many people conclude that all you have to do is invest a few bucks in motion picture deals and you'll make a fortune! Certainly not. *Titanic* is the exception to the rule and losing money is not very much fun, even if your name appears on the silver screen. Most individual investors have lost money in films.

✔ One risk to a film is timing. When your movie is in the screenplay phase, the concept may be popular, but by the time the film is released, the public's whims may have changed and your film may be out of favor. Remember it takes more than a year from start to finish to make a typical film.

✔ Will the stars, who may have been very popular/*bankable* before you started shooting, be as popular when the film is released, or has their popularity begun to fade?

bankable   from the standpoint of film deals, a bankable star or personality would be one who has successfully drawn a crowd to previous films, made money over the years for various movie companies by appearing in their films, and whose name, when associated with a new film project, lends a comfort level to the people financing the deal. The bankable star's participation acts as a form of collateral for the investors.

✔ Did the film come in under budget, or were cost overruns so high that the picture has to be seen by nine out of ten moviegoers just to break even?

✔ Were there enough investors putting in sufficient capital to finish the film, or did additional capital have to be raised during production (under less favorable terms, obviously), thereby diluting your initial interest and compromising your ultimate return?

✔ Was the project completed within enough time to assure release during a prime season (Christmas, over the summer, etc.) when the maximum audience is available to buy tickets?

✔ Are the critics (who are frequently wrong) doing handstands well before release, or are they panning this project during the early shooting stages?

All of the above factors, coupled with accounting practices that are not understood by motion picture industry members, much less the general investing public, make putting your dollars into such deals pure speculation and only to be pursued with 100 percent risk capital. If you happen to hit a winner, great, but don't count on spending those profits until you have the money in your hand. And don't forget the fact that if you are invited to invest in one of these deals, it probably means that the industry experts feel that the project is too risky or too small to warrant them risking their capital. In these cases, you probably should not invest your money in the film project in the first place.

OTHER DEALS THAT LACK ECONOMIC SUBSTANCE

Lack of economic substance mainly applies to pure speculative deals and tax shelters. Regardless of the investment program, the key is that the business fundamentals are intact and there is at least a reasonable likelihood that you will make money. Sometimes neighbors, peers, coworkers, classmates, nephews, nieces, or grandchildren want you to fund their latest venture, which is sure to make you a millionaire. These ventures can work and are usually extremely exciting. But, most of these schemes lose money. Be very careful with your money.

RESEARCH AND DEVELOPMENT (R&D) DEALS AND COMPANIES

Basic research is at best a very long and drawn out process and most projects don't result in a marketable product or drug or development. You should consider any money that you put into this group as very low on your list of priorities. This is pure 100 percent high-risk capital. Certainly, there may be some tax advantages and other write-offs associated with the investment available to you over time, but these need to be assessed by your personal tax adviser as they apply to your tax needs and position. If you are just investing for the tax advantages, you might want to look elsewhere.

On the brighter side of this issue, some of the companies devoted to research and development have actively traded stocks on various exchanges, and some are even included in the more aggressive or aggressive/growth biotech mutual fund portfolios. If this is the case, even if nothing marketable comes out of the research being done immediately, while the stock is in the news, being recommended by brokerage firms, and included in those mutual fund portfolios, there will be lots of trading activity and there may exist opportunities for shorter-term trading profits. That is not to say that this would eliminate the risk of ownership and the possibility of ultimate losses. Look at the company's *annual report* and *prospectus* and see just how many projects are under development and how many dollars have already been devoted to research. If both of these areas are full of activity, the risk factor would be somewhat lower.

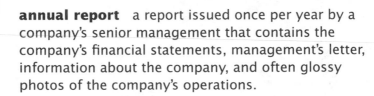

annual report   a report issued once per year by a company's senior management that contains the company's financial statements, management's letter, information about the company, and often glossy photos of the company's operations.

prospectus   a printed description of an enterprise that is distributed to prospective buyers; in the case of securities, a summary of the registration statement filed with the SEC that explains the nature of the security being offered to the public.

VENTURE CAPITAL

Start by thinking of getting together with three or four coworkers for the purposes of pooling your money and buying a lottery ticket. This is perhaps the purest form of venture capital and represents the maximum risk being taken. The four of you invest equal amounts of money into a deal that if it works would multiply your original investment 10 or 20 times. But if the investment fails, you will lose all your collective capital. Of course, in this deal there is no management to consider as a risk factor, no inventions or developments to be perfected and later marketed, no possible need for additional capital; and the "security" purchased is totally unmarketable.

If you view venture capital from the above point of view, you cannot get hurt.

Whatever the nature of the deal, it has to be operated by someone. Do the principals have any experience in this or that field and are they the least bit familiar with the ins and outs of marketing, hiring additional qualified people, borrowing additional capital, putting in 80 or more hours a week to make it work, and so on. These are just a few of the considerations to be addressed before you write that venture capital check. What percentage of the company will you own? Will the company be borrowing the money from you while it grows and will it be able to pay you interest and ultimately repay all money borrowed at some point in time? What is the likelihood the company will require additional subsequent investments to get the concept off the ground? Still more considerations.

Are you looking to put money into a deal that is part of a huge industry populated by giants with endless financing to compete against, or is your company one of a few in this arena developing a new product, formula, or service altogether? If most of these questions can be answered favorably, the risk faced isn't 100 percent; but if not, all of the dollars you "venture" into this project will probably be lost, and therefore, again, only 100 percent risk capital should be put into venture capital deals.

We touched on the lack of marketability as it relates to investments into venture type situations. Perhaps the company in question is already a small public entity and is traded on NASDAQ or some regional exchange. These facts would take a little more of the risk away from venture capital deals because there would, at least, be someplace to sell that stock if you wanted to liquidate your investment sooner rather than later. But, obviously, as the situation fails to develop, the products don't find a ready market, or the new wonder drug remains in the approval stage at the Food and Drug Administration (FDA) for an endless review period, even that limited marketability would be compromised as well.

ASSETS INELIGIBLE FOR INSURANCE COVERAGE AGAINST DISASTER

Some assets are not insurable. This means that you are at risk for 100 percent of your investment in the face of a natural disaster. As wonderful as that dream villa you own on the Bay of Naples, in the shadow of Mount Vesuvius may seem, or how valuable that hillside dream house, that overlooks San Francisco-by-the-Bay, right smack on the San Andreas Fault may be, or how marvelous any other property is that you have in the vicinity of typhoon activity, tornadoes, hurricanes, or other serious storm activity, you probably cannot purchase commercial disaster insurance. These assets, which you are most likely carrying on your personal family *balance sheet* at current market value, may be worthless in the event one of the above "disasters waiting to happen" occurs.

> **balance sheet**   statement of financial condition: assets owned, liabilities owed, and the shareholders' equity.

Just calculate your risk if that villa in Naples, which today is valued at $250,000 and carries a $150,000 mortgage, were to be buried by a volcanic eruption. Not only wouldn't you have a villa or its remains to resell, but also you would still owe the balance of that mortgage. A scenario like this is quite possible.

Is your vacation home in Hawaii? Near Mount Fuji in Japan? In the tornado belt in our own Southern states? On any of the Pacific islands that regularly experience typhoon activity? Or anywhere else of a similar nature?

Those assets, which cannot be covered by disaster insurance, are at as much risk as they are worth. Can you afford to lose that much? If so, fine, keep them and hope no disaster will occur. Otherwise, sell these properties now and reinvest your money elsewhere.

DERIVATIVES

We included derivative type securities in both Chapters 5 and 6 because under the circumstances described they could be considered either low-risk assets or medium-risk assets. We include them yet again here under high-risk assets for some of the following reasons. (Reread Chapters 5 and 6 as they apply to the risks involved in each of those cases).

Keeping in mind that derivative securities are created securities whose value depends on the value of the securities they were created from, it should be obvious that the nature of the underlying securities will determine just how risky the derivative will be. Obviously, those securities created from/based on the stocks of the Dow Jones Industrial Average (the DIAMONDS) and those based on the S&P 500 Index (the SPDRs) (both of these derivatives were discussed earlier in Chapters 5 and 6) would be only as risky as the underlying securities, whose quality and trading history are well known.

On the other hand, we see emerging a world of derivative securities based on issues of a lesser quality, shorter track record, poorer dividend payout history, more sporadic earnings, and lower or no ratings from the recognized rating services. These more speculative derivative securities belong in the high-risk category, only to be invested in with dollars that can be lost. Their value may be far too volatile and their resale far too uncertain for them to be included among the medium-risk assets.

LOTTERIES, CASINOS, AND OTHER GAMBLING

Many individuals play the lotteries or visit casinos. Consider the recent Powerball lotteries where several states pool their lotteries to create a megajackpot worth over $100 million. The odds of winning such a lottery can be 1 in 80 million. While many people spend only a few dollars for a ticket, the risks are enormous because the probability of winning is so low. Consider these games to be games of chance and high risk.

Chapter

8

Mutual Funds and Asset Allocation

Mutual funds are a popular way to invest today. There are over 8000 mutual funds in existence. While selecting a specific mutual fund may be tricky, mutual funds provide an ideal way to help you meet your asset allocation objectives.

MUTUAL FUNDS DEFINED

A *mutual fund* is a pool of money that is managed by an investment professional. The investment professional or money manager researches companies and investments. The manager purchases and sells investments in accordance with the mutual fund's investment objectives and investment policies.

> **mutual fund**   pool of money managed by an investment professional.

PERSONAL INVESTMENT OBJECTIVES

A successful financial plan begins with investment goals and objectives. As discussed earlier in this book, investment objectives may include capital appreciation, current income, and preservation of capital. Once you establish investment objectives, you can select the proper mix of assets (asset allocation) and then specific investments to achieve your investment objectives.

Mutual Funds Come in All Shapes and Sizes

✔ Money markets.

✔ Municipal bonds.

✔ U.S. Treasury bills.

✔ U.S. Treasury notes and bonds.

✔ Corporate bonds (short-, intermediate-, and long-term).

✔ Junk or high-yield bonds.

✔ International or foreign bonds.

✔ Common stocks (blue-chip, mid-cap, small-cap, sector funds).

✔ International or foreign stocks.

✔ Real estate investment trusts (REITs and mutual funds of REITs).

✔ Commodities (gold, silver, other minerals).

MUTUAL FUND OBJECTIVES

United States–based mutual funds are governed by the *Securities and Exchange Commission (SEC)*. The SEC requires each mutual fund to prepare a prospectus at least once per year and whenever a major change to the fund's investment policies and practices occurs. Among other things, the prospectus explains the mutual fund's investment objectives and investment policies.

securities and exchange commission (SEC)   the U.S. governmental agency that governs the U.S. securities markets and the securities industry; established in 1934.

For example, a money market mutual fund's objective is likely to be "invest in highly rated (high-quality), short-term investments with the objective of preserving principal and earning the highest yield possible."

In contrast, a capital appreciation common stock mutual fund's objective may be "invest in common stocks with the objective of increasing the value of the investments."

It is important to read a mutual fund prospectus to determine whether the mutual fund's investment policies mesh with your investment objectives. Once you invest in a mutual fund, it is important to review the prospectus every year and monitor the fund's investments in order to ensure that the fund still meets your objectives.

MUTUAL FUNDS AS AN ALLOCATION TOOL

Mutual funds offer a convenient way to allocate your money to your investment categories. Once you establish a financial plan, write down your target asset allocation percentages and the types of investments you want to make in order to implement your financial plan.

Then select those mutual funds whose stated investment objectives match your asset allocation program. Suppose your investment portfolio equals $100,000 (we chose this number for illustration purposes and to simplify the math) and your asset allocation entails investing 60 percent of your money ($60,000) in common stocks. Within that framework, you might decide to invest 45 percent of $60,000 in blue-chip or large-cap common stocks, 15 percent in foreign stocks, 20 percent in income-producing common stocks such as real estate companies and utilities, and 20 percent in small-cap common stocks.

Table 8.1 is an illustrative portfolio of common stocks allocated among different types of common stocks. In this example, 100 percent or $60,000 represents the entire investment in common stocks, which equals 60 percent of the total portfolio of $100,000.

TABLE 8.1 Common Stock Sample Allocation		
Type of Common Stock	Percentage of Total Investment in Common Stocks	Dollar Investment
Blue-chips	45%	$27,000
Foreign stocks	15	9,000
Income-producing stocks	20	12,000
Small-caps	20	12,000
Totals	100%	$60,000

The asset allocation featured in Table 8.1 is an example and may or may not be suitable for you.

SELECTING MUTUAL FUNDS

Once you select your asset allocation, you should select mutual funds that follow your stated objectives. For large-cap or blue-chip stocks, you might select a large-cap growth or value fund or an S&P 500 Index fund. You can learn more about mutual funds by reading mutual fund analyses in the *Wall Street Journal*, *Investor's Business Daily*, the *New York Times*, *Morningstar Mutual Funds*, and other financial publications.

OVERLAPPING ALLOCATIONS AND SIMPLICITY

Many times, different investments, including mutual funds, overlap. For example, blue-chip common stocks typically pay dividends. In the example, we selected a mutual fund that invests in blue-chip common stocks and a fund that invests in income-producing common stocks. It is possible that both of these mutual funds invest in utilities. In such cases, you may find that your allocation is somewhat different from your intended allocation because the mutual fund portfolio manager may buy securities that are outside your target allocation. In the interest of simplicity and efficiency, select your allocations and your investments but don't go overboard with too many narrow categories. Take a reasonable approach to asset allocation.

MUTUAL FUNDS VERSUS INDIVIDUAL SECURITIES

The decision to invest in mutual funds versus individual securities is outside the scope of this book. However, as discussed earlier, it is important to view your asset allocation across all of your money and investments. You may own individual common stocks as well as mutual funds that invest in common stocks, plus shares of your company stock through your employer-sponsored retirement plan or an employee profit sharing or stock purchase plan. All of these investments represent shares of common stock, regardless of the form of ownership.

For example, if you are an employee of a publicly traded company, possibly you participate in the company's employee stock purchase program or the company's match to your 401(k) retirement plan is in the form of company stock. You should consider these investments as part of your overall asset allocation.

Similarly, you may decide to maintain a certain maximum percentage (asset allocation) of your portfolio in your company's stock. When you review your brokerage and retirement plan statements, it should be clear how many shares of company stock you own. But don't narrow your review to just those statements. Consider company stock you own or control in all forms. You may also own restricted shares or preferred shares. You may be a participant in a profit sharing plan that is tied to the company's stock performance. Your bonus may be payable in company stock. Perhaps you own options. In addition, you may own mutual fund shares that invest in your company stock. You may own or control more shares of your company's stock than you think.

With mutual funds, it is sometimes difficult to monitor your actual specific asset allocations. The mutual fund portfolio manager may buy or sell shares of your company stock. Or, the manager may change the portfolio in light of his or her view of the market, and this may alter your actual investment allocation. On a practical basis, it is almost impossible to lock in an exact asset allocation. And this should be okay, as asset allocation is a blueprint for success.

MUTUAL FUNDS FOR DIVERSIFICATION

In Chapter 1, we discussed the difference between allocation and diversification. Once you establish a target asset allocation, you can select mutual funds or individual securities, or a combination of both, to help you achieve your financial goals. Mutual funds invest in a particular type of security, and this helps you to implement your asset allocation program. Please do not confuse this with diversification.

Mutual funds help to diversify your investments within an investment class. A mutual fund is a pool of money that the portfolio manager invests in a number of securities. For example, a mutual fund may hold as few as 30 to 40 different securities or as many as 200 to 300 different securities. This diversification helps you to minimize investment or unsystematic risk.

MUTUAL FUND ASSET ALLOCATION
VERSUS DIVERSIFICATION

When you select an asset allocation, once you decide to invest through mutual funds, you should select the best mutual fund in an asset class. Keeping in mind that mutual funds by their nature provide diversification, you should select only one mutual fund in a particular class. Owning two blue-chip common stock mutual funds, one S&P 500 Index mutual fund, and one large-cap common stock value mutual fund is essentially making four similar investments. These investments are highly correlated, meaning that the securities in the portfolio move in the same direction. This violates the principles of asset allocation, which are designed to smooth out your investments such that one portion of your portfolio increases in value at the same time other portions of your portfolio stay the same or decline in value.

LIFE CYCLE OR COMBINATION MUTUAL FUNDS

Many mutual fund families offer combination mutual fund products. These funds are essentially "funds of funds." They are designed to provide one-stop asset allocation programs. For example, the Vanguard Group (1-800-662-7447) offers LIFEStrategy portfolios. At one time, the Vanguard LIFEStrategy Growth Portfolio held 20 percent bonds and 80 percent stocks. The Vanguard LIFEStrategy Income Portfolio held 20 percent reserves (money market instruments), 20 percent stocks, and 60 percent bonds. T. Rowe Price (1-800-541-6128) as well as other mutual fund families offer similar products.

These funds are designed to allow you to make one investment and implement your asset allocation program. These products can be effective, especially when you have only enough money to invest in one mutual fund. On the other hand, when you decide to establish your own asset allocation, you should consider selecting individual mutual funds instead of a fund of funds.

HOW MANY MUTUAL FUNDS TO OWN

We have worked with people who have invested in 15 or 20 different mutual funds. In most of these cases, these people held several mutual funds that invested in the same investment classes (i.e., the same types of securities). Numerous studies have shown that investing in different mutual funds that pursue the same investment objectives can have a detrimental effect on your wealth. The success of one portfolio manager is likely to cancel out the success of the other portfolio managers, and your returns are likely to approach the average.

If you invest in one mutual fund that is the top performer in its investment category, your other mutual fund investments are likely to reduce your overall returns. One mutual fund manager might invest in the top-performing common stock in the pharmaceuticals industry. The other mutual fund managers might invest in common stocks of different pharmaceutical companies and these investments may post lower investment returns or even losses. The performance of the top investment will be offset by the poor performance of the other investments.

✔ Select the mutual fund in a particular category with the best five-to-ten-year history of top performance.

✔ Select one mutual fund for each investment category to meet your asset allocation program.

✔ Consider mutual fund costs, fees, and expenses.

✔ Own no more than eight mutual funds.

Suppose a married couple participates in their 401(k) retirement plans. Both plans offer an S&P 500 Index mutual fund and both spouses invest in the S&P 500 Index fund. Keep in mind that the plans are separate so each spouse must make investments in his or her respective plan. While this represents two mutual fund investments, these investments should be exactly the same since they follow the same methodology. One exception might be different expenses charged by each fund.

MUTUAL FUNDS: ADDED REWARDS

Mutual funds offer many benefits and rewards, especially for patient investors.

✔ *Easy Investment.* Mutual fund sponsors make it relatively easy to invest in their mutual funds. You can complete a straightforward two-page application and include a personal check.

✔ *Small Dollars.* Many mutual funds have low initial and small continuing minimum investment requirements. Some mutual funds have $1000 minimums for regular accounts and $500 minimums for individual retirement accounts. Other fund sponsors require no initial investment as long as you commit to invest at least $50 or $100 per month automatically from your checking account.

✔ *Diversification.* Mutual funds offer diversification in that you can pool your relatively small sum of money with other people's money for the mutual fund manager to invest in numerous different securities. This smooths out your returns.

✔ *Professional Money Management.* Mutual fund families hire investment advisers and professional portfolio managers who research companies and follow the securities markets on a daily basis.

✔ *Recordkeeping.* Mutual fund sponsors maintain detailed records about the fund and your account and prepare monthly, quarterly, or semiannual account statements. Statements of some funds, such as T. Rowe Price, help you determine the taxable capital gain or loss when you sell your mutual fund shares.

✔ *Daily Tracking.* Most newspapers print daily mutual fund results so you can monitor your mutual fund performance.

MUTUAL FUNDS: ADDED RISKS

✔ *Fees and Expenses.* Mutual funds charge a variety of fees and expenses. Typically, these expenses are charged as a percentage of assets under management. These expenses and charges include management fees, *12b-1 fees* for marketing, and sometimes *sales charges* or *loads*. These fees and expenses increase as the dollars in the mutual fund increase. In recent years, investors have poured more and more money into mutual funds and the bull market has swelled the dollars in a mutual fund. Since the fees and charges are a percentage of the assets under management, the fees and charges you pay increase as the assets in the fund increase.

12b-1 fees fees deducted from a mutual fund's assets to compensate the mutual fund sponsor or broker-dealer for marketing the fund.

sales charges fees charged to buy and sell mutual funds (aka loads).

✔ *Lack of Your Control over Investment Choices.* Once you invest in the mutual fund, you delegate all the money management responsibilities, including investment selection, to the portfolio manager. The only way you can control your investment choices is to sell your mutual fund shares.

> **loads** fees or sales commissions paid for the purchase of mutual funds. Generally, the traditional load or sales charge to purchase a mutual fund is 8.5 percent of the purchase price. A load of less than 8.5 percent indicates a low-load fund; in some cases there is no up-front sales charge, and we have what is known as a no-load fund. Also known as the sales charge or the commission.

✔ *Inability to Control Your Tax Position.* By law, mutual funds are required to distribute the net capital gains and dividends to their shareholders every year. The portfolio manager decides which securities to invest in and sell. The manager's actions determine your tax bill. Holding individual securities helps you manage your income taxes because you can determine whether to hold or sell a security.

✔ *Size That Makes a Difference.* When a mutual fund's assets exceed $2 billion, it can become difficult for the portfolio manager to beat the S&P 500 Index. When a fund is relatively small, the returns on each particular stock have a more significant impact on the returns of the overall fund.

✔ *Run on the Fund.* In the event the investors in a mutual fund (or individual securities for that matter) decide to withdraw their money from the fund, depending on how much idle cash the mutual fund holds, the portfolio manager may have to liquidate (sell) other holdings to meet the redemptions. This can cause you to lose money as the value of your mutual fund shares may decline, or you may realize capital gains on which you'll have to pay income taxes.

CONCLUSION

Mutual funds can offer an excellent way to invest your money and build wealth. What's more, mutual fund families offer many products that invest in specific securities or types of securities. And this can be an ideal way for you to implement your asset allocation strategy.

Chapter

Retirement Planning

In this chapter, we discuss planning for retirement and ideas and action steps designed to help you achieve your retirement goals.

RETIREMENT OBJECTIVES

Success generally involves setting goals and objectives. Once you establish a target, you can establish a plan and take action steps to achieve your goals. Living a comfortable retirement and building wealth to achieve that goal are not exceptions to that rule. Before you can effectively create a financial plan and an asset allocation for your retirement portfolio, you must decide what kind of retirement life you would like to lead.

Consider these factors:

✔ When would you like to retire: 55? 60? 65?

✔ Where would you like to live?

✔ How much would you like to travel?

✔ What extra costs will you face during retirement: supporting your parents? children? grandchildren?

✔ Do you have a family history of any diseases? Will they require costly treatment?

✔ How many years do you expect to live after you retire?

✔ How old are you now?

✔ How much money can you save and invest now during your working years to build wealth for retirement?

Your objectives coupled with the above-mentioned factors will help you determine how much money you will need for your retirement living expenses and how much wealth you will need to accumulate to achieve that standard of living. The first step is to assign a dollar value to your spending habits.

RETIREMENT TRENDS

In the United States, there are four major trends regarding retirement that impact retirement planning:

1. Citizens are living longer.
2. Retirees are leading more active lives.
3. More people are starting families later in life.
4. More people have to fund their own living expenses in retirement.

Increased Life Expectancy

Your life expectancy, coupled with when you intend to retire and how much retirement assets (sources of income) you have accumulated, will help you determine how much money you need to fund your retirement. Average life expectancy has increased, but an average is one's age based on the statistics of a large number of people. You may be above or below average. The best way to determine your life expectancy is to review your family history and visit your doctor.

We recommend that in general people manage their money based on a life expectancy of 100. This age is chosen for several reasons. First, as life expectancy continues to increase, it is conceivable that more people will live to age 100 and will need their money for at least that long. Second, making your money last longer helps you in the event your actual spending exceeds your budget, your actual returns on investment are less than your expected returns, or you incur unforeseen medical or other expenses.

According to the U.S. National Center for Health Statistics,* in 1970 U.S. males had an average life expectancy of 67.1 years and females had an average life expectancy of 74.7 years. By 1995 the average life ex-

*U.S. Bureau of the Census, *Statistical Abstract of the United States: 1997* (117th edition), Washington, DC, 1997.

pectancy of U.S. males had increased to 72.6 years and the average life expectancy of females had increased to 78.9 years.

Based on the life expectancy statistics, the trend is that people are living longer. This has two interesting implications regarding retirement:

✔ Because we are likely to live longer than prior generations, our retirement lives are likely to be longer.

✔ We will need more resources to live comfortably throughout our lifetimes.

In effect, if we live longer, we need more resources to support ourselves. To generate incremental wealth, it is crucial to begin saving and investing money as early as possible in your working years. If you are in your 20s, this would be an ideal time to begin saving for retirement. If you are 30 or older, don't delay; begin right away.

You can build more wealth by:

✔ Dedicating a larger percentage of your income to your investment programs.

✔ Spending less money.

✔ Planning your career wisely to maximize your wealth and employee benefits.

✔ Delaying retirement for a year or two or three.

✔ Embarking on a new part-time career today to save more money.

✔ Embarking on a new part-time career in retirement.

✔ Assuming more risk in your investment portfolio with the objective of increasing your returns and your wealth.

Retirees More Active

In 1970 when men's life expectancies were 67.1 years, if a man retired when he was 62 or 65 years old, on average he needed funds for only 5 years. Over time, new pharmaceuticals and medical procedures, better health care, better diets, and a shift away from manual labor have led to increased life expectancy.

Today, assuming a man retires at age 62 and has a life expectancy of 72.6 years, he can expect 10 years in retirement. Since people today retire at a relatively younger age than prior generations, today's retirees are likely to lead more active lives. This may include playing more golf and tennis and traveling. In addition to funding leisure activities, it is likely that your health-care costs will increase over time. These factors imply that we will need more money over time to live comfortably.

More People Start Families Later in Life

Today, a greater percentage of the population attends college and graduate school, and more couples are dual-income couples. While both people are earning a salary, they may have to devote a relatively large portion of their income to servicing their student loans. To the extent people begin their careers later in life, they are more likely to earn a relatively lower salary than prior generations who began their careers five or ten years earlier. This can delay the amount of disposable income they can devote to retirement savings.

Generally, people are getting married and having children later in life. If a couple has a child when they are 20 years old, on average the child will graduate from college 22 years later when the parents are 42 years old. Today, if a couple has a child when they are 30 to 35 years old, on average they will be 52 to 57 years old when the child graduates from college. These demographics change people's income and the savings and investment profile of today's population. As a result of these factors and, of course, your personal circumstances, it is important to manage your money accordingly.

Fund Your Own Retirement

Today, there is an increasing shift toward people having to fund their own retirement. In the past, most companies and especially unionized organizations paid retirees a fixed amount of money starting when they reached age 62 or 65 and continuing for the remainder of their lives. These pension plans are called *defined-benefit plans*. The payout or pension benefit is a defined-amount of dollars.

> **defined-benefit plans**   the payout or pension benefit is defined in dollars.

Pension plans of today are typically *defined-contribution plans*. In defined contribution plans the company contributes a specific or defined amount of money into your pension account and you are responsible for managing your own money. The sum total value of your retirement account assets equals the money you can use to support yourself. Often, the company makes a contribution to your retirement account equal to a percentage of your salary or a percentage match. Under a match, your employer may double your contributions to your retirement account, up to perhaps 5 percent of your salary. Under some plans, the company makes its matching contribution in the company's common stock. The company's matching contribution may not vest (be yours) for four or five years.

defined-contribution plans   the company contributes a specific or defined amount of money into your pension account today and you are responsible for managing your own money.

In addition, Social Security benefits seem to make up a smaller percentage of our retirement income over time.

These factors and trends mean we must assume greater responsibility for our financial health during our working years and retirement lifetime.

PROJECTING RETIREMENT INCOME

A rule of thumb is to project your highest salary and increase that amount by 3.1 percent for inflation for each year between now and when you intend to retire. If you are 52 years old today, plan to retire in 3 years at age 55, and currently earn a salary of $100,000, you may want to plan to spend $109,591 in pretax income during your retirement. (See Table 9.1.) This formula is designed to preserve your purchasing power in light of the effects of inflation. In other words, you will lose 3.1 percent of your money to inflation every year. You can make this calculation with a financial calculator or computer spreadsheet program.

TABLE 9.1 Accounting for Inflation			
Year	Beginning Amount	Inflation Factor	Ending Amount
1	$100,000	3.1%	$103,100
2	103,100	3.1	106,296
3	106,296	3.1	109,591

Projected Sources of Income

Potential sources of retirement income were discussed in Chapter 4. Most of these sources are self-explanatory, but a few of them are worth discussing further. The next few paragraphs explore a few points about retirement sources of income.

Defined-Benefit Pension Plans. These plans require the payer to pay the retiree a sum of money regularly for the rest of his or her life. This sum or pension benefit is a fixed amount of money. This amount may or may not meet your income and spending objectives; you may have to accumulate additional wealth to meet your objectives. Also, since these amounts are fixed dollars, your pension benefits lose a percentage of their purchasing power every year. These benefits are based on complicated formulas that include your ending salary and years of service or tenure with the company. They also vest (become yours to keep) after a certain number of years of service—typically five years. After this time, you are entitled to receive the benefits even if you leave the company. It is important to understand your company's rules and policies so you can factor these benefits into your planning.

For example, if your pension benefits vest after five years and you have worked with the company for four years, you may want to remain with the company for at least another year before resigning to take another job. It is also worthwhile to analyze the financial strength and stability of the company. While the Pension Benefit Guaranty Corporation (PBGC) governs pension rules and establishes requirements for U.S. companies and their pension plans, a number of U.S. companies have unfunded pension obligations (the amount the company owes the plan) that exceed the pension plan assets (investments). This case does not necessarily mean you'll lose your retirement benefits, but the more investments the pension plan has compared to its pension payout obligations the safer the plan is. Of course, there are many other factors involved here such as the nature of the investments (allocation) the pension assets are invested in.

Defined-Contribution Retirement Plans. Under these programs, the individual is responsible for building wealth for his or her retirement. This means you probably have to contribute a portion of your current paycheck to your retirement account, and you have to select investments; hence, the importance of asset allocation.

Income from Sale of Residence. This source of income assumes you sell your primary residence and buy a less expensive home. This may or may not be a realistic assumption for you. You should forecast the current and expected fair market value of your home (you can call your local Realtor). This number provides an estimate of the sales proceeds you should receive; remember to factor in selling costs, which equal approximately 3 percent to 10 percent of the value of your home. Also, consider how much debt you owe against your home; this includes mortgages, home equity loans, and home equity lines of credit. Then, the other key point here is that you move and purchase a less expensive home.

Downsizing. This is also called life simplification. In effect, you trim your expenses by cutting back. We have counseled people who have sold a relatively large house to move to a smaller ranch house. These people also sold one of their two cars and sold their boat. In the process, the selling price of the larger home exceeded the purchase price of the smaller home. They freed up capital for spending and investing.

Inheritances. The likelihood of receiving an inheritance can be a very complex and sensitive subject. In addition to the personal sensitivity people have about dying, wills, and passing on their money to heirs, on a practical basis, there is the question about the probability of receiving any inheritance, and how much. One relatively conservative approach is to assume that your relatives will outlive their money and you'll receive no inheritance. You should probably allocate your money and investments accordingly.

TAX-ADVANTAGED RETIREMENT PROGRAMS

As defined-contribution plans have overtaken defined-benefit plans, tax-advantaged programs have become more commonplace. Tax-advantaged retirement plans include:

- ✔ Individual retirement accounts (IRAs).
- ✔ Roth IRAs.
- ✔ 401(k) plans.
- ✔ 403(b) plans.
- ✔ 457 plans.
- ✔ Nondeductible IRAs (Form 8606; contributions are made in after-tax dollars and income accumulates tax-free until withdrawal).

Under some of these plans, individuals can contribute money to their retirement plans on a pretax basis, receive a current income tax deduction equal to their contribution, earn tax-deferred income until they make withdrawals, and take advantage of company matching contributions where offered.

In 1998, for example, the U.S. government established that the maximum annual contribution to an individual's 401(k) retirement account is the lower of either that individual's taxable salary income or $10,000. You will receive a current income tax deduction equal to 100 percent of your qualifying contributions.

There are restrictions on contributions to qualifying plans, penalties and income taxes associated with withdrawals if you are younger than $59\frac{1}{2}$ (except in certain limited circumstances), and mandatory withdrawals when you reach age $70\frac{1}{2}$. As with all tax-based investing programs, it is worthwhile to consult your employee benefits department, your financial adviser, or your tax adviser.

EMPLOYER MATCHING CONTRIBUTIONS

In many plans, employers match a percentage of the employee's retirement plan contributions. For example, your employer may match 100 percent of your contributions up to 5 percent of your salary. If you earn $100,000 in salary income and you contribute $5,000 to your retirement plan account, under this example, your employer would contribute an additional $5,000 to your retirement plan account. Keep these points in mind:

✔ The matching contribution can represent a 100 percent return on your investment.

✔ Whenever practical, contribute enough money to your account to collect the maximum employer matching contribution.

✔ The employer matching contribution may vest (become yours) over time.

✔ If the employer pays the matching contribution in company stock, this is likely to affect your asset allocation.

TAX-DEFERRED ANNUITIES

Tax-deferred annuities have become a particularly popular investment product in the past 10 years. Under a tax-deferred *annuity*, investors make contributions in after-tax dollars and the income accumulates tax-free until they make withdrawals. Like the retirement plans already discussed, withdrawals are taxable at ordinary income tax rates. But unlike those plans, withdrawals become mandatory only when you reach 85 years of age.

> **annuity** a payment stream over a period of time, usually from an insurance company.

Tax-deferred annuities come in two general varieties: fixed and variable. Under a fixed annuity, the sponsor agrees to pay a fixed rate of interest on your money. Under a variable annuity, the sponsor invests your money in a portfolio of common stocks, often the S&P 500 Index, and the actual rate of return on the portfolio determines your payout.

Under both types of annuities, you can select a point in time when you want to begin receiving payments. This is called annuitization. The sponsor is likely to offer you several payout options that are designed based on your life expectancy. Usually the payments stop when you die, but one exception to this is when you elect to receive payments based on your and your spouse's life expectancy; the payments will be lower, but the surviving spouse continues to receive benefits for the remainder of his or her life. Under most annuities, if you die prematurely, any remaining benefits are lost. Under other programs, your estate receives a death benefit based on the money remaining in your account.

Tax-deferred annuities can be a helpful financial planning and investment tool. Unfortunately, though, tax-deferred annuities typically carry higher fees and expenses than the typical mutual fund. In order to achieve the tax deferral of the income, the tax-deferred annuity contains an insurance policy in addition to the investment portfolio. This tends to add an additional layer of costs over the conventional mutual fund product. What's more, many times tax-deferred annuities are sold by financial planners who charge a sales commission. Typically, there are also steep surrender charges if you terminate the tax-deferred annuity before seven years.

Most magazines and the *Wall Street Journal* rank annuities. Vanguard Mutual Funds (1-800-662-7447), T. Rowe Price (1-800-541-8318), and Scudder (1-800-225-2470) also offer popular annuity products. Consult current annuity rankings and track records, and check with your financial planner before opening such an account.

It is typically more advantageous to postpone investing in a tax-deferred annuity in order to take advantage of the other tax-advantaged plans mentioned earlier in this chapter. This is particularly the case when you can participate in your company-sponsored 401(k) plan or 403(b) plan where your employer matches a portion of your contributions. Also, the Roth IRA may be more powerful for you than a tax-deferred annuity, depending on your tax position.

TIME HORIZON

Earlier in this chapter we discussed your retirement objectives, in particular when you want to retire. The implication is that you have only a certain number of years remaining in the workforce. This is important for two reasons: First, you will have that many years in which to contribute money to your retirement account, and second, once you begin making withdrawals, you lose some of the power of compound returns.

Depending on how long your time horizon is and how much wealth (retirement assets) you have accumulated to date compared to your retirement goal, you may have to adjust your plan. Consider the following:

✔ Defer your retirement for a year or two or three in order to leave your money intact to grow.
✔ Save and invest more money today.
✔ Scale back your retirement lifestyle.
✔ Invest somewhat more aggressively in hopes of achieving higher returns and therefore building more wealth.
✔ Embark on a new career in retirement.

Your decisions regarding these factors will help you establish your asset allocation. Certainly, the sooner you begin investing for retirement, the less you have to invest in order to accumulate a specific amount.

PORTFOLIO THEORY

Perhaps by now you have developed an idea about how you would like to allocate your assets. In Chapter 4 we discussed two points that are relevant to retirement planning. First, retirement assets are generally long-term assets. Your time horizon or investment period hopefully will be long, especially if you begin saving and investing money at a relatively young age. Second, over the long run—15 to 20 years—the volatility associated with common stocks tends to disappear and the returns approach the long-term averages. Depending on your self-examination and your personality profile, in many ways the most reasonable place to weight your portfolio toward common stocks and other equities is in your retirement accounts.

Over the long run, common stocks have outperformed other classes of investments. The return on the Standard & Poor's 500 stock index was 11.0 percent from 1926 to 1997. (Used with permission. © 1998 Ibbotson Associates, Inc. All rights reserved.) See Chapters 3 and 4 for more data on rates of return. If the long run averages continue into the future, then common stocks will continue to outperform other classes of investments. Nonetheless, based on available data and historic rates of return, it seems that everyone should commit at least some percentage of their assets to common stocks and other growth-oriented assets. We cover this topic in Chapters 10 through 14 where we profile different life stages.

Single People

PROFILE

The single people group includes people who have never married or never teamed up with a partner, those who are widowed or divorced, and those who are widowed or divorced with children. A member of this group typically:

- ✔ Is 18 to 34 years old or older.
- ✔ Is developing a first or perhaps second career.
- ✔ Is post–high school, college, graduate school.
- ✔ May live at home with parents or rent or own an apartment or a house.
- ✔ May own or lease a car.
- ✔ Is likely to have incurred debt under student loans.
- ✔ Possibly incurred debt on credit cards.
- ✔ Is beginning to invest money.

Single people fall into two groups: those who expect to marry or partner up, and those who never marry or who are divorced or widowed and do not remarry. The main theme for these people is establishing a lifestyle and a financial plan. This probably entails paying off student loans and then buying a home and saving for retirement. It is important to get a handle on your expenses and likely lifetime income so you can balance your spending and your saving and investing. As a single person, your cost of living is likely to be lower than as a family, but you lose certain economies of scale such as insurance and the cost of housing.

Those people who are divorced or widowed with children face a special set of issues and concerns. From a financial standpoint, they may or may not pay or receive alimony or insurance. Divorce tends to be a major adjustment on both an emotional and a financial level. Financially, in the past the couple was ostensibly working towards a common set of goals. Now, the couple has split up into two distinct households. One spouse may pay the other spouse alimony. Alimony is typically payable monthly or quarterly and is payable over a specified period of time or term. After that time, the alimony payments stop. This has important implications regarding personal spending. An important issue regarding wealth is the status and ownership of retirement plan assets. Hopefully, you and your attorney considered these factors when you negotiated your divorce settlement. Another important factor is the home. In the past, the woman often ended up keeping the former family residence and the male spouse moved out. Depending on your settlement, your financial position, and your family status, you may want to sell your home and move to a different house or neighborhood. Housing and where to raise a family comprise a particularly complicated subject that overarches the financial aspects of home ownership.

Divorced with children presents an entirely new dimension to one's life. First, hopefully there are child support payments. Second, there is the adjustment relating to breaking up a marriage and a household. Third, there is custody of and visitation with the children. The parent with custody is likely to be somewhat burdened with the day-to-day care of the children as well as having to work. A dual-income home is the norm today, so this may not represent an adjustment. The parent with visitation rights and the parent with custody must work out how and when the children will see the noncustodial parent. Often, the parent who lives with the children in some ways becomes both the father and the mother. This can be enormously difficult, especially considering the financial aspects of raising a family and establishing a new life for yourself. Fourth, there is the possibility of a second marriage and perhaps children from the new spouse's prior marriage or newborns together with that spouse.

FINANCIAL OBJECTIVES

- ✔ Establishing a lifestyle.
- ✔ Establishing a profession/career.
- ✔ Becoming a family.

✔ Building wealth.

✔ Saving for retirement.

✔ Making the transition from child to adult.

✔ Supporting yourself and your family.

✔ Reducing your debt.

✔ Buying or leasing a car.

✔ Buying a home.

✔ Furnishing your residence.

✔ Funding college for yourself.

✔ Saving for college for your children.

OPPORTUNITIES

✔ Invest early and consistently to build wealth.

✔ Start to invest early to take advantage of compound returns.

✔ Save money before you have children and incur other fixed costs.

✔ Establish a lifestyle and fixed cost base that you can afford.

✔ Become an educated consumer of financial products.

✔ Learn how to manage your money.

✔ Plan for your future wisely.

✔ Balance spending, saving and investing.

✔ Begin saving for retirement.

✔ Take advantage of employer-sponsored retirement programs.

✔ Reduce debt relatively early.

✔ Manage your spending and avoid credit card debt.

✔ Pay off your credit card debt before it multiplies and you begin to rely on the funds.

✔ Plan your career for the long run.

✔ Typically, you can assume a relatively large degree of risk and recover from mistakes and failures.

RISKS

✔ Spending too much money.

✔ Incurring fixed costs at an unmanageable level.

✔ Incurring too much consumer debt.

✔ Failing to save and invest money.

✔ Thinking you will postpone saving for your future until you earn more money.

✔ Failing to establish goals and objectives.

✔ Failing to establish a financial plan.

✔ Failing to implement your financial plan.

✔ Failing to get a handle on your transition to adulthood, especially divorced with children.

TIME HORIZON AND PLANNING

The time horizon for this group is relatively long—hopefully 60 to 80 years or so. The key is to establish a financial plan and use your money wisely. Almost all of us earn a relatively fixed income. And most of us can reasonably project our lifetime income. The authors have counseled professionals including doctors and lawyers who have earned significant six-figure incomes and have faced financial difficulties. Primarily, these people have embarked on a lifestyle that is well beyond their means. They purchase magnificent homes and expensive cars. They take lavish vacations. These people establish a lifestyle and a fixed cost base that consumes almost all of or more than their income. Over time, their spending tends to spiral out of control, they incur consumer debt that they cannot pay off, and they are unable to invest money for their future. It is always wiser to adopt a relatively conservative lifestyle, and as your income and wealth grow you can purchase a more expensive home or car. Begin building your base and establish the foundation for building wealth as early as possible.

Asset allocation is important, and the younger you are and the longer your time horizon, the more important it is to consider investing a greater percentage of your money in common stocks and other assets that have the potential to appreciate in value. As a member of this group, you are likely to face various financial needs, including retiring student and perhaps credit card debt, buying a house or apartment, buying or leasing an automobile, and investing for retirement. It is worthwhile to balance your objectives and your spending. For example, it would be wise to start saving some money for your retirement today, especially if your employer offers a retirement plan and matches a percentage of your contributions. This is the case even if you have student loans. It is also helpful to segregate your money into different pools to achieve specific objectives. You may channel a portion of your income to retire your student loans and credit card debt. You may need a car to commute to work, so you may need to save money immediately to make a down payment for an automobile. You may want to purchase a home within five years, so this is a relatively short-term goal. The key is to assess your financial goals and plan your life and your finances accordingly.

INVESTMENT OPPORTUNITIES

- ✔ Investing in assets that have a high probability to grow (capital appreciation), especially since you should have a relatively long time horizon to recover from any losses.
- ✔ Building a base in your portfolio. One way to accomplish this goal is to invest in a blue-chip common stock mutual fund or a mutual fund that invests primarily in common stocks that have a long-standing history of paying quarterly dividends and raising their dividends.
- ✔ Starting your own business. When most people are relatively young they can recover from most financial losses and they have flexibility. In other words, they are likely to have relatively few responsibilities and financial obligations and can manage their expenses to start a business.

Consider investing some money in a high-quality blue-chip common stock mutual fund or closed-end mutual fund that has a top track record and pays a relatively high dividend.

Closed-end mutual funds trade on the New York Stock Exchange or other stock exchanges. Closed-end mutual funds have mixed track records, especially compared to many of the S&P 500 Index mutual funds. However, closed-end mutual funds that pay a relatively high annual dividend offer both capital appreciation and a base for your portfolio and wealth-building program. The shares of a closed-end mutual fund trade at a premium or discount to the value of the securities owned by the portfolio. Suppose a closed-end mutual fund trades at $10 per share on the New York Stock Exchange and the *net asset value (NAV)* of the portfolio equals $12 per share. This fund trades at a 16.67 percent discount to net asset value. Consider funds that trade at a relatively steep discount to their net asset value and that are at a relative low to their historic discount. If you invest in a closed-end mutual fund, reinvest your distributions and purchase additional shares in the fund.

> **net asset value (NAV)**   the fair market value of the securities held by the mutual fund. NAV is often calculated as follows: fund's assets minus fund's liabilities divided by mutual fund shares.

Consider investing a portion of your portfolio in high-risk assets. In particular, consider mutual funds that concentrate on high-technology, health care, and biotechnology companies. Typically, these investments are fairly volatile but offer relatively high growth opportunities.

INVESTMENT RISKS

- ✔ Not investing in assets that offer capital appreciation.
- ✔ Investing too much money in low-yielding assets such as money market instruments, certificates of deposit (CDs), and U.S. Treasury securities.
- ✔ Investing too much money in high-risk assets such as options, futures, venture capital, and other hit-or-miss investments.

TABLE 10.1 Sample Target Asset Allocation Percentages for Single People	
Asset Category	*Allocation Percentages*
Cash and equivalents	0 to 5
Fixed-income investments	5 to 10
Blue-chip common stocks	50 to 70
Foreign blue-chip common stocks	10 to 15
Small-capitalization common stocks	0 to 10
Medium-risk assets not covered above	5 to 10
High-risk assets	0 to 5

Note: The target percentages add up to more or less than 100 percent at each end of the ranges because different people are likely to allocate their money in different ways across asset categories.

ASSET ALLOCATION

Table 10.1 and Figure 10.1 present a range of target asset allocations—the percentage of your money that you might want to allocate to each investment category. It is crucial that you consider these target percentages as a sample illustration and that you consider them in light of your own personal objectives and circumstances. Be sure to consult with your financial professionals and advisers. At the very least, use these allocations as a benchmark or comparison tool for your current asset allocation. You may be assuming too much or too little risk based on your needs and circumstances.

If you are selecting fixed-income investments, you may want to select a mix of high-grade (investment-grade) corporate bonds, high-yield bonds (junk bonds), and perhaps U.S. Treasury bonds or municipal bonds, depending on your income tax rate. It is often wise to invest in bonds that mature in 10 years or less.

Medium-risk assets may include real estate investment trusts (REITs) or other investment properties.

Your asset allocation may change depending on the stability and level of your income, the debt service payments you must make, and the amount of money you need to support your family. For example, a divorced parent who is responsible for paying children's expenses may need to adopt a relatively conservative investment program and asset allocation in order to accumulate more money for emergencies and unforeseen costs and expenses. But in the retirement plan assets, divorced parents may

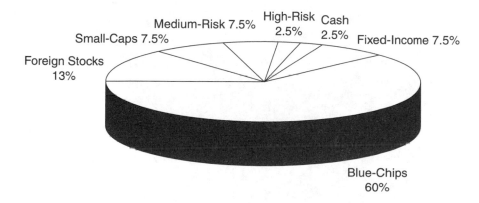

FIGURE 10.1   Sample target asset allocation based on ranges in Table 10.1.

want to emphasize common stocks to grow their assets, especially if their current contributions are limited by family expenses.

Asset Allocation Pie Chart

The pie chart in Figure 10.1 represents only one combination of asset allocation. You may choose an entirely different asset allocation based on your needs and objectives.

Young Married Couples

PROFILE

The young married group includes people who recently married. Members of this group typically:

- ✔ Are 26 to 35 years old.
- ✔ Are melding the lives of two different people.
- ✔ Are becoming a nuclear family.
- ✔ Are bringing two extended families together.
- ✔ Are joining finances.
- ✔ Are merging investment styles and financial priorities and objectives.
- ✔ Are establishing a financial plan and investment program.
- ✔ Are developing a first or perhaps second career.
- ✔ Are post–high school, college, graduate school.
- ✔ Rent or own an apartment or a house.
- ✔ May own or lease one or two cars.
- ✔ Are likely to have incurred debt under student loans and be paying down the debt.
- ✔ Possibly are considering graduate school.
- ✔ Possibly incurred debt on credit cards.
- ✔ Are beginning to invest money.

This stage of life is typically characterized by two distinct people with two different upbringings and sets of values joining together. There is often an adjustment period because different people may have contrasting views and perspectives on how to manage money, and different risk tolerance, investment strategy, and lifestyle. It is very important to work together to compromise and develop one financial plan or two compatible plans.

FINANCIAL OBJECTIVES

- ✔ Establishing a lifestyle together as a couple.
- ✔ Establishing professions/careers.
- ✔ Seeking promotion and status in careers.
- ✔ Becoming a family.
- ✔ Building wealth.
- ✔ Saving for retirement.
- ✔ Making the transition from single adults to couple.
- ✔ Supporting your family.
- ✔ Reducing your debt.
- ✔ Buying or leasing one or perhaps two cars.
- ✔ Buying a home.
- ✔ Furnishing your residence.
- ✔ Paying down your student loans.

OPPORTUNITIES

- ✔ Invest early and consistently to build wealth.
- ✔ Start to invest early to take advantage of compound returns.
- ✔ Save money before you have children and incur other fixed costs.
- ✔ Establish a lifestyle and fixed cost base that you can afford that takes into account the needs, comfort level, and objectives of the couple.
- ✔ Become an educated consumer of financial products.
- ✔ Learn how to manage your money.
- ✔ Plan for your future together wisely.
- ✔ Balance spending, saving, and investing.

✔ Analyze each spouse's assets and liabilities.

✔ Analyze each spouse's financial opportunities—for example, employee benefits such as retirement plans, insurance programs, and health insurance.

✔ Save for retirement.

✔ Take advantage of employer-sponsored retirement programs.

✔ Reduce debt relatively early.

✔ Manage your spending and avoid credit card debt.

✔ Pay off your credit card debt before it multiplies and you begin to rely on the funds.

✔ Plan your career for the long run.

✔ Typically, you can assume some degree of risk and recover from mistakes and failures.

RISKS

✔ Failing to collaborate to form a financial plan.

✔ Spending too much money.

✔ Incurring fixed costs at an unmanageable level.

✔ Incurring too much consumer debt.

✔ Failing to save and invest money.

✔ Thinking you will postpone saving for your future until you earn more money.

✔ Failing to establish goals and objectives.

✔ Failing to implement your financial plan.

✔ Failing to get a handle on your transition to being a couple, especially divorced with children.

TIME HORIZON AND PLANNING

The time horizon for this group is relatively long—hopefully 60 years or so. The key is to establish a financial plan together as a couple and use your money wisely. This does not necessarily mean that you should merge all of your assets into joint accounts. Initially, it can be beneficial to keep those assets that each of you entered into the marriage with in separate accounts. Over time as you grow closer together and solidify your marriage and your nuclear family, you can merge your assets. Merging assets can have a number of consequences, including estate tax consequences. Consult your financial adviser and estate planner.

Financial planning is especially important at this major transition point in your lives. Two people are now together. Each spouse may have grown up in different family environments with varied socioeconomic backgrounds, opposing views and perspectives on managing money, diverse ideas and habits about spending, saving, and investing money. For some couples, discussing money management and financial planning can be a sensitive and emotional topic. If this is the case with you, consider seeking the help of a financial planner or adviser.

Hopefully, both of you have managed your money wisely and have begun saving for the future. When two people get married, they typically buy a home and one or two cars. Some people already own these assets before they get married, but many couples consider these assets to be a relatively near-term goal. Of course, with a new home comes the desire to furnish that home. These expenditures are relatively major dollar amounts and require saving and planning.

Almost all of us earn a relatively fixed income. And most of us can reasonably project our lifetime income. Once you establish your retirement lifestyle and financial objectives, you can plan ahead and invest wisely. It is always wiser to adopt a relatively conservative lifestyle, and as your income and wealth grow you can upgrade your lifestyle. Begin building your base and establish the foundation for building wealth as a couple, as early as possible in your marriage.

Asset allocation is important, and the younger you are and the longer your time horizon, the more important it is to consider investing a greater percentage of your money in common stocks and other assets that have the potential to appreciate in value. This is important, especially if you hope to have children. While people's incomes tend to rise over time, children are costly. From the first days of life, they need food, clothing, and medical care. Over time, you may have to fund costs relating to child care, schooling, and extracurricular activities, such as sports, dance, religious school, and hobbies. If you analyze your personal life horizon and plan accordingly, you can channel a relatively large portion of your current income to build your investment portfolio today. This way, when your out-of-pocket expenses rise and you may want to reduce your contributions to your investment portfolio, your portfolio can continue to grow, intact. This way, you take advantage of compound returns.

As a member of this group, you are likely to face various financial needs including retiring student loans and perhaps credit card debt, buying a house or apartment, buying or leasing an automobile, and investing for retirement. It is worthwhile to balance your objectives and your spending. For example, it would be wise to save some money for your retirement today, especially if your employer offers a retirement plan and matches a percentage of your contributions. If both spouses work, each spouse should contribute a percentage of his or her income to his or her retirement plan. This is essential to your long-term financial success. Be sure to take advantage of employer matching contributions.

Trim your living expenses so that you use one spouse's salary, overtime, and bonus to fund daily living expenses and the other spouse's salary to reduce consumer and student loan debt and invest for the future.

It is also helpful to segregate your money into different pools to achieve specific objectives. You may channel a portion of your income to retire your student loans and credit card debt. You may need a car and you may want to purchase a home in three to five years; these are relatively short-term goals. You may hope to have children at some point in time. The key is to assess your financial goals and plan your life and your finances accordingly.

INVESTMENT OPPORTUNITIES

- ✔ Investing in assets that have a high probability to grow (capital appreciation), especially since you should have a relatively long time horizon to recover from any losses.

- ✔ Building a base in your portfolio. One way to accomplish this goal is to invest in a blue-chip common stock mutual fund or a mutual fund that invests primarily in common stocks that have a long-standing history of paying quarterly dividends and raising their dividends.

- ✔ Starting your own business. When they are relatively young, most people can recover from any losses and they have flexibility. In other words, they are likely to have relatively few responsibilities and financial obligations and can manage their expenses to start a business. If both spouses work outside the home, one spouse could start a business while the other maintains a more stable job that provides a relatively steady income.

Consider investing some money in a high-quality blue-chip common stock mutual fund or closed-end mutual fund that has a top track record and pays a relatively high dividend.

Closed-end mutual funds trade on the New York Stock Exchange or other stock exchanges. Closed end mutual funds have mixed track records, especially compared to many of the S&P 500 Index mutual funds. However, closed-end mutual funds that pay a relatively high annual dividend offer both capital appreciation and a base for your portfolio and wealth building program. The shares of a closed-end mutual fund trade at a premium or discount to the value of the securities owned by the portfolio. Suppose a closed-end mutual fund trades at $10 per share on the New York Stock Exchange and the net asset value of the portfolio equals $12 per share. This fund trades at a 16.67 percent discount to net asset value. Consider funds that trade at a relatively steep discount to their net asset value and that are at a relative low to their historic discount. If you invest in a closed-end mutual fund, reinvest your distributions and purchase additional shares in the fund.

Regardless of your wealth and risk tolerance, consider investing a portion of your portfolio in high-risk assets. In particular, consider mutual funds that concentrate on high-technology, health-care, and biotechnology companies. Typically, these investments are fairly volatile but offer relatively high growth opportunities. This segment of your portfolio can boost your overall rate of return.

INVESTMENT RISKS

✔ Not considering each spouse's objectives, investment style, and risk tolerance.

✔ Not investing in assets that offer capital appreciation.

✔ Postponing investing until you become more established financially and as a married couple. Even if you are anxious about physically merging your financial assets, each spouse can continue to build wealth by funding his or her own retirement plan.

✔ Investing too much money in low-yielding assets such as money market instruments, CDs, and U.S. Treasury securities.

✔ Investing too much money in high-risk assets such as options, futures, venture capital, and other hit-or-miss investments.

ASSET ALLOCATION

Table 11.1 and Figure 11.1 present a range of target asset allocations—the percentage of your money that you might want to allocate to each investment category. It is crucial that you consider these target percentages as a sample illustration and that you consider them in light of your own personal objectives and circumstances. Be sure to consult with your financial professionals and advisers. At the very least, use these allocations as a benchmark or comparison tool for your current asset allocation. You may be assuming too much or too little risk based on your needs and circumstances.

If you are selecting fixed-income investments, you may want to select a mix of high-grade (investment-grade) corporate bonds, high-yield bonds (junk bonds), and perhaps U.S. Treasury bonds or municipal bonds, depending on your income tax rate. It is often wise to invest in bonds that mature in 10 years or less.

Medium-risk assets may include real estate investment trusts (REITs) or other investment properties.

Your asset allocation may change depending on the stability and level of your income, the debt service payments you must make, the amount of money you need to support your family, and the time horizon for your objectives. For example, if you want to buy a home or car, these may be relatively short-term goals and you may want to channel a large

TABLE 11.1 Sample Target Asset Allocation Percentages for Young Married Couples	
Asset Category	*Allocation Percentages*
Cash and equivalents	0 to 5
Fixed-income investments	5 to 15
Blue-chip common stocks	40 to 75
Foreign blue-chip common stocks	10 to 15
Small-capitalization common stocks	0 to 10
Medium-risk assets not covered above	5 to 10
High-risk assets	0 to 7.5

Note: The target percentages add up to more or less than 100 percent at each end of the ranges because different people are likely to allocate their money in different ways across asset categories.

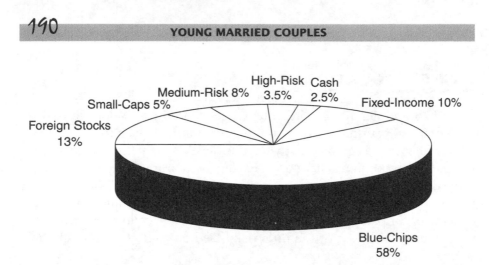

FIGURE 11.1 Sample target asset allocation based on ranges in Table 11.1.

portion of your income into relatively low-risk assets for these purposes. Even if you set aside money for a down payment on a home or car, you should still participate in a retirement plan for the future. You should also consider establishing a small fund for emergencies and unforeseen costs and expenses.

Asset Allocation Pie Chart

The pie chart in Figure 11.1 represents only one combination of asset allocation. You may choose an entirely different asset allocation based on your needs and objectives.

Married with Children

PROFILE

This group includes married couples who have one or more children. Members of this group typically:

- ✔ Are 28 to 42 years old.
- ✔ Are building a nuclear family.
- ✔ Are transitioning from a married couple of two to a family of three or more.
- ✔ Possibly are still joining finances.
- ✔ Possibly are merging investment styles and financial priorities and objectives.
- ✔ Are establishing a financial plan and investment program.
- ✔ Are facing changing spending patterns and household expenses due to children.
- ✔ Are funding child care and education costs.
- ✔ Are analyzing whether both spouses will continue to work outside the home or whether one spouse will leave the workforce to care for the children.
- ✔ Are advancing in a first career or perhaps embarking on a second career.
- ✔ Are post–high school, college, graduate school.
- ✔ Rent or own apartment or a house.

✔ Own or lease one or two cars.

✔ Are likely to have incurred debt under student loans and be paying down the debt, or to have retired the student loans.

✔ Possibly incurred debt on credit cards.

✔ Are investing money for retirement.

This stage of life is typically characterized by a married couple expanding into a larger nuclear family with one or more children. There is often an adjustment period because people have varied views and perspectives on how to manage money, risk tolerance, investment strategy, and lifestyle. It is very important to work together to compromise and develop one financial plan or two compatible plans.

FINANCIAL OBJECTIVES

✔ Establishing a lifestyle together as a couple with children.

✔ Advancing in professions/careers.

✔ Seeking promotion and status in careers.

✔ Becoming a family with children.

✔ Building wealth.

✔ Saving for retirement.

✔ Making the transition from a couple to a couple with children.

✔ Supporting your now larger family.

✔ Reducing your debt.

✔ Buying or leasing one or perhaps two cars.

✔ Buying a home.

✔ Furnishing your residence.

✔ Paying down your student loans.

✔ Paying down credit card debt.

✔ Funding expenses of your children and infants.

OPPORTUNITIES

✔ Invest early and consistently to build wealth.

✔ Continue to take advantage of compound returns.

✔ Save money in advance to plan for increased costs and expenses associated with your children.

✔ Establish a lifestyle and fixed cost base that you can afford that takes into account the needs, comfort level, and objectives of the couple and how you want to raise your children.

✔ Become an educated consumer of financial products.

✔ Learn how to manage your money in light of your growing family.

✔ Plan for your larger family's future wisely.

✔ Balance spending, saving, and investing.

✔ Analyze whether both spouses will continue to work outside the home.

✔ Analyze each spouse's financial opportunities—for example, employee benefits such as retirement plans, insurance programs, and health insurance.

✔ Continue to save for retirement in light of increased family expenses.

✔ Take advantage of employer-sponsored retirement programs.

✔ Continue to reduce debt.

✔ Manage your spending and avoid credit card debt.

✔ Pay off your credit card debt before it multiplies and you begin to rely on the funds.

✔ Plan your career for the long run.

✔ Typically, you can assume a smaller degree of risk than in earlier life stages because your spouse and now your children rely on you for financial support.

RISKS

✔ Failing to form a financial plan.

✔ Failing to implement your financial plan.

✔ Spending too much money.

✔ Not planning for increased expenses relating to children.

✔ Incurring fixed costs at an unmanageable level.

✔ Incurring too much consumer debt.

✔ Failing to save and invest money.

- ✔ Thinking you will postpone saving for your future until you earn more money and become comfortable with the increased family expenses.
- ✔ Failing to establish goals and objectives.
- ✔ Failing to get a handle on your transition to being a couple with children.
- ✔ Failing to write a will and estate plan. In particular, it is crucial to appoint a guardian for your children.

TIME HORIZON AND PLANNING

The time horizon for this group is relatively long—hopefully 50 years or so. The key is to establish a financial plan together as a couple and use your money wisely. This does not necessarily mean that you should merge all of your assets into joint accounts. Initially, it can be beneficial to keep those assets that each of you brought into the marriage in separate accounts. Over time as you grow closer together and solidify your marriage and your nuclear family, you can merge your assets. Merging assets can have a number of consequences, including estate tax consequences. Consult your financial adviser and estate planner.

Trim your living expenses so that you use one spouse's salary, overtime, and bonus to fund daily living expenses and the other spouse's salary to reduce consumer and student loan debt and invest for the future. Or, one spouse can leave the workforce to care for the children.

INVESTMENT OPPORTUNITIES

- ✔ Investing in assets that have a high probability to grow (capital appreciation), especially since you should have a relatively long time horizon to recover from any losses.
- ✔ Building a base in your portfolio. One way to accomplish this goal is to invest in blue-chip common stock mutual fund or a mutual fund that invests primarily in common stocks that have a long-standing history of paying quarterly dividends and raising their dividends.
- ✔ Starting your own business. When they are relatively young, most people can recover from any losses and they have flexibility. In other words, they are likely to have fewer responsibilities and

financial obligations and can manage their expenses to start a business. If both spouses work outside the home, one spouse could start a business while the other maintains a more stable job that provides a relatively stable and steady income. But, you may have to scale back your plans to start a business if your children need your steady income for living expenses.

Consider investing some money in a high-quality blue-chip common stock mutual fund or closed-end mutual fund that has a top track record and pays a relatively high dividend.

Closed-end mutual funds trade on the New York Stock Exchange or other stock exchanges. Closed-end mutual funds have mixed track records, especially compared to many of the S&P 500 Index mutual funds. However, closed-end mutual funds that pay a relatively high annual dividend offer both capital appreciation and a base for your portfolio and wealth building program. The shares of a closed-end mutual fund trade at a premium or discount to the value of the securities owned by the portfolio. Suppose a closed-end mutual fund trades at $10 per share on the New York Stock Exchange and the net asset value of the portfolio equals $12 per share. This fund trades at a 16.67 percent discount to net asset value. Consider funds that trade at a relatively steep discount to their net asset value and that are at a relative low to their historic discount. If you invest in a closed-end mutual fund, reinvest your distributions and purchase additional shares in the fund.

Consider investing a portion of your portfolio in high-risk assets. In particular, consider mutual funds that concentrate on high-technology, health-care, and biotechnology companies. Typically, these investments are fairly volatile but offer relatively high growth opportunities. As you advance to other life stages, you may want to commit a smaller percentage to these relatively risky asset categories and focus more on assets that provide capital appreciation and pay current dividends.

INVESTMENT RISKS

✔ Not considering each spouse's objectives, investment style, and risk tolerance.

✔ Not investing in assets that offer capital appreciation

✔ Postponing investing until you become more established financially and as a married couple. Even if you are anxious about physically merging your financial assets, each spouse can continue to build wealth by funding his or her own retirement plan.

✔ Investing too much money in low-yielding assets.

✔ Investing too much money in high-risk assets such as options, futures, venture capital, and other hit-or-miss investments.

✔ Not carrying adequate insurance policies.

✔ Not making a will and not selecting a guardian for your children.

ASSET ALLOCATION

Table 12.1 and Figure 12.1 show a range of target asset allocations—the percentage of your money that you might want to allocate to each investment category. Consider these target percentages as a sample illustration and consider them in light of your own personal objectives and circumstances. Be sure to consult with your financial professionals and advisers. At the very least, use these allocations as a benchmark or comparison tool for your current asset allocation. You may be assuming too much or too little risk based on your needs and circumstances.

If you are selecting fixed-income investments, you may want to select a mix of high-grade (investment-grade) corporate bonds, high-yield bonds (junk bonds), and perhaps U.S. Treasury bonds or municipal

TABLE 12.1 Sample Target Asset Allocation Percentages for Married Couples with Children	
Asset Category	*Allocation Percentages*
Cash and equivalents	0 to 7.5
Fixed-income investments	5 to 25
Blue-chip common stocks	40 to 70
Foreign blue-chip common stocks	10 to 15
Small-capitalization common stocks	0 to 7.5
Medium-risk assets not covered above	5 to 10
High-risk assets	0 to 5

Note: The target percentages add up to more or less than 100 percent at each end of the ranges because different people are likely to allocate their money in different ways across asset categories.

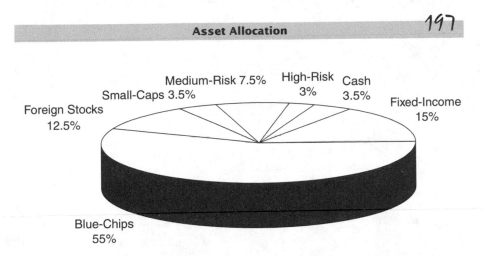

Medium-Risk 7.5% High-Risk Cash
Small-Caps 3.5%   3%   3.5%
Foreign Stocks   Fixed-Income
12.5%   15%
Blue-Chips
55%

FIGURE 12.1 Sample target asset allocation based on ranges in Table 12.1.

bonds, depending on your income tax rate. It is often wise to invest in bonds that mature in 10 years or less.

Medium-risk assets may include utilities, real estate investment trusts (REITs), or other investment properties.

Your asset allocation may change depending on the stability and level of your income, the debt service payments you must make, the amount of money you need to support your family, and the time horizon for your objectives. For example, there are the medical costs associated with having a child and the costs of furnishing a child's room including crib and buying a high chair, car seat, and so on. If you want to buy a larger home or a new or second car, these may be relatively short-term goals and you may want to channel a large portion of your income into relatively low-risk assets for this purposes. Even if you face higher family expenses and out-of-pocket costs, you should still participate in a retirement plan for the future. With a growing family, it becomes more important to establish a fund for emergencies and unforeseen costs and expenses or at least a credit line where you can borrow money on relatively short notice.

Asset Allocation Pie Chart

The pie chart in Figure 12.1 represents only one combination of asset allocation. You may choose an entirely different asset allocation based on your needs and objectives.

Chapter 13

Couples Saving for College and Retirement

PROFILE

This group includes people who are married, have children, and are primarily focused on accelerating their wealth building efforts for their children's college education and for their own retirement. A member of this group typically:

✔ Is 30 to 55+ years old.

✔ Has a nuclear family where the children are at least 5 years old.

✔ Is reaching peak earning years.

✔ Is reviewing financial goals.

✔ Is analyzing portfolio: assets, success, and future needs.

✔ Is adjusting financial plan and investment program.

✔ Is facing changing spending patterns and household expenses due to children's college tuition bills rapidly approaching.

✔ Is analyzing whether the spouse who may have left the workforce to care for the children will return to the workforce to accelerate savings and investment.

✔ Is advancing in a first or second career or perhaps embarking on a second or third career.

✔ Rents or owns an apartment or a house.

✔ Takes one or more vacations per year.

✔ Owns or leases one or two cars.

✔ Is likely to be paying down the home mortgage debt and perhaps the remaining balances under student loans.

✔ Possibly incurred debt on credit cards.

✔ Is investing money for retirement.

✔ Is investing money for college tuition and related expenses.

This stage of life is typically characterized by a married couple planning for the next stage of life, which is the children going to college and the couple emphasizing investing for their own retirement.

FINANCIAL OBJECTIVES

✔ Establishing a lifestyle that takes into account the likely income level of the couple.

✔ Advancing in professions/careers.

✔ Seeking promotion and status in careers.

✔ Building wealth for retirement.

✔ Building wealth to fund college tuition.

✔ Saving for retirement.

✔ Making the transition from a couple with young children to a couple with children who are on their way to college.

✔ Reducing your debt.

✔ Buying or leasing one or perhaps two cars.

✔ Perhaps buying or leasing a car for your children.

✔ Buying a home or vacation home.

✔ Paying down credit card debt.

OPPORTUNITIES

✔ Invest consistently to build wealth for retirement.

✔ Accelerate investments to tax-advantaged retirement programs.

✔ Continue to take advantage of compound returns.

✔ Save money in advance to plan for increased costs and expenses associated with your children's anticipated college expenses.

✔ Review your lifestyle and fixed cost base to determine whether your spending levels are too high in light of your desire to help fund your children's college expenses and your desire to live a comfortable retirement.

✔ Become an educated consumer of financial products.

✔ Focus on how you can adjust your financial plan and portfolio to take advantage of income tax benefits and incentives.

✔ Arrange your finances to minimize estate taxes.

✔ Learn how to manage your money in light of your new objectives.

✔ Balance spending, saving, and investing.

✔ Analyze whether the spouse who may have left the workforce years ago to raise the children will return to the workforce.

✔ Analyze each spouse's financial opportunities—for example, employee benefits such as retirement plans, insurance programs, and health insurance.

✔ Continue to save for retirement in light of increased family expenses.

✔ Take advantage of employer-sponsored retirement programs.

✔ Continue to reduce debt, especially the home mortgage.

✔ Manage your spending.

✔ Avoid credit card debt.

✔ Pay off your credit card debt before it multiplies and you begin to rely on the funds.

✔ Plan your career for the long run.

✔ Typically, you can assume a smaller degree of risk than in earlier life stages because your spouse and now your children rely on you for financial support.

RISKS

✔ Failing to form a financial plan.

✔ Failing to implement your financial plan.

✔ Spending too much money.

✔ Not planning for increased expenses relating to children's tuition.

✔ Being unrealistic about how much money you need to save for retirement.

✔ Continuing to incur fixed costs at an unmanageable level.

✔ Continuing to incur too much consumer debt.

✔ Failing to save and invest enough money to achieve your goals.

✔ Thinking you will postpone saving for your future until you earn more money.

✔ Failing to establish a new financial plan in light of your revised goals and objectives.

✔ Failing to carry enough insurance.

✔ Failing to update your will and estate plan. It is particularly important to appoint a guardian for your children.

One risk today for this age group is having to care for and support your children and possibly your parents and grandparents. This is often called the "sandwich generation"—you are in the middle of the sandwich because you are between two generations: You are providing financial support to your children and perhaps other generations, at the same time. This situation becomes particularly complex from a financial standpoint. Depending on how many assets the older generation has, an enormous strain can be put on your own finances and financial position. Plan accordingly and seek professional financial advice as early as possible.

Another risk you may face is planning for elder or long-term care. Unfortunately, many companies have curtailed or eliminated postretirement medical benefits. Former employees are now responsible for funding a higher percentage of their medical costs and expenses once they retire. Again, plan ahead and seek professional financial advice early.

Depending on your financial position and how important it is to you to help fund your children's college expenses, you may want to encourage your children to get jobs and save money to fund at least a portion of their college costs.

TIME HORIZON AND PLANNING

The time horizon for this group is relatively long—hopefully 30 to 50 years or so. At this point in your lives, it should be clear what your income prospects will be throughout the remaining years of your career. Depending on where you are today in relation to achieving your financial goals and objectives, you may want to change your current lifestyle in order to maximize the likelihood you will achieve your long-range goals, especially living a comfortable retirement.

Financial planning is especially important at this point in your lives. First, you are probably reaching or may have entered your peak earning years. Your children are getting older and are approaching college age. Each spouse may have his or her own views and perspectives about how much money to save for the children's college education and how much current income to channel toward saving and investing for the couple's future.

This stage in your life offers you the opportunity to capitalize on your hopefully relatively high annual income and channel more money into your investment portfolio. On the one hand, a relatively high level of income and relatively low or stable fixed costs should enable you to save money for your children's education. On the other hand, once you analyze the value of your investment portfolio and consider its current value in relation to the likely growth of your investments and your retirement needs, you may want to channel more of your current income into your portfolios for future growth. Your children can borrow money to fund tuition and are likely to be in a better position to pay off those student loans than you can.

The authors have counseled people who earned significant incomes and underestimated their likely financial needs in retirement and the amount one needs to invest during working years in order to build enough wealth to fund the desired retirement lifestyle. Many people establish a lifestyle and a fixed cost base that consumes almost all or even more than their income. If you have done this, you may want to take this opportunity to trim your expenses and put extra money toward reducing any consumer debt you have incurred and beefing up your investments.

Asset allocation is important at this life stage as well as in earlier stages. Even if you are 50 years old, it is likely that you will live for another 25 to 35 years. This means that you still need to grow your portfolio, and capital appreciation is an important component of your financial well-being. The younger you are and the longer your time horizon, the more important it is to consider investing a greater percentage of your money in common stocks and other assets that have the potential to appreciate in value and serve as a potential hedge against inflation. This is important, especially if you hope to live in retirement for at least 20 years.

While people's income tends to rise over time, their costs and expenses tend to rise over time as well. If you analyze your personal life horizon and plan accordingly, you can channel a relatively large portion of your current income to build your investment portfolio today, especially if you have not invested enough money in the past. This way, you can still take advantage of compound returns and income tax deferral. You still have time to build wealth for retirement, although not as much time as in earlier life stages. As you get older, it becomes more and more important to adopt a more conservative stance and take action to build enough wealth for retirement. But it is always important to grow your assets (capital appreciation).

As a member of this group, you are likely to face various financial needs, including funding some of your children's college expenses, perhaps servicing credit card debt, and investing for retirement. It is worthwhile to balance your objectives and your spending. For example, it would be wise to save a larger portion of your income today for your retirement. Reexamine your employee benefits and in particular any vesting periods regarding pensions, Social Security benefits, and postretirement medical benefits. You may want to continue working with your present company for the vesting period before switching to a new employer.

It is also helpful to segregate your money into different pools to achieve specific objectives. It is likely that you will want to channel a portion of your income to fund money for your children's college education and to fuel your investment portfolios. The key is to assess your financial goals and plan your life and your finances accordingly.

Trim your living and discretionary expenses so that you can channel a greater percentage of your current income to fund college savings programs and increase your retirement assets. Pay down as much debt as possible to reduce your fixed obligations and your interest expense.

INVESTMENT OPPORTUNITIES

✔ Investing in assets that have a high probability to grow (capital appreciation). You should probably emphasize higher-quality and more reliable assets that pay consistent dividends and other distributions and still offer growth potential. Depending on your income level, your net worth, and your time horizon, you may have a relatively long period to recover from any losses.

✔ Increasing your base in your portfolio that will provide significant current income later on, particularly when you retire. One way to accomplish this goal is to invest in a blue-chip common stock mutual fund or a mutual fund that invests primarily in common stocks that have a long-standing history of paying quarterly dividends and raising their dividends.

✔ Splitting your portfolio into two components: one for your children's college education and one for your own retirement. It is likely that the investment time horizon for college expenses will be shorter than the horizon for your retirement assets.

Consider investing some money in a blue-chip capital appreciation fund or a closed-end mutual fund that has a top track record and pays a relatively high dividend.

Closed-end mutual funds trade on the New York Stock Exchange or other stock exchanges. Closed-end mutual funds have mixed track records, especially compared to many of the S&P 500 Index mutual funds. However, closed-end mutual funds that pay a relatively high annual dividend offer both capital appreciation and a base for your portfolio and wealth building program. The shares of a closed-end mutual fund trade at a premium or discount to the value of the securities owned by the portfolio. Suppose a closed-end mutual fund trades at $10 per share on the New York Stock Exchange and the net asset value of the portfolio equals $12 per share. This fund trades at a 16.67 percent discount to net asset value. Consider funds that trade at a relatively steep discount to their net asset value and that are at a relative low to their historic discount. If you invest in a closed-end mutual fund, reinvest your distributions and purchase additional shares in the fund.

As you advance to this life stage and future life stages, you should commit a smaller and smaller percentage to relatively risky asset categories and focus more on assets that offer capital appreciation and pay current dividends.

INVESTMENT RISKS

✔ Not considering each spouse's objectives, investment style, and risk tolerance.

✔ Not investing in assets that offer capital appreciation.

✔ Not controlling your costs and expenses.

✔ Not investing aggressively enough to meet your retirement needs.

✔ Saving too much money for your children's college education at the expense of saving for your own retirement.

✔ Postponing investing for yourself until you finish funding your children's college education.

✔ Investing too much money in low-yielding assets such as money market instruments, certificates of deposit, and U.S. Treasury securities.

✔ Investing too much money in high-risk assets such as options, futures, venture capital, and other hit-or-miss investments.

✔ Not carrying adequate insurance policies.

✔ Not updating your will.

ASSET ALLOCATION

Table 13.1 and Figure 3.1 present a range of target asset allocations—the percentage of your money that you might want to allocate to each investment category. It is crucial that you consider these target percentages as a sample illustration and you consider them in light of your own personal objectives and circumstances. Be sure to consult with your financial professionals and advisers. At the very least, use these alloca-

TABLE 13.1 Sample Target Asset Allocation Percentages for Married Couples Saving Money for Their Own Retirement and for Their Children's College Education	
Asset Category	*Allocation Percentages*
Cash and equivalents	0 to 15
Fixed-income investments	10 to 30
Blue-chip common stocks	40 to 55
Foreign blue-chip common stocks	7.5 to 10
Small-capitalization common stocks	0 to 5
Medium-risk assets not covered above	5 to 10
High-risk assets	0 to 2.5

Note: The target percentages add up to more or less than 100 percent at each end of the ranges because different people are likely to allocate their money in different ways across asset categories.

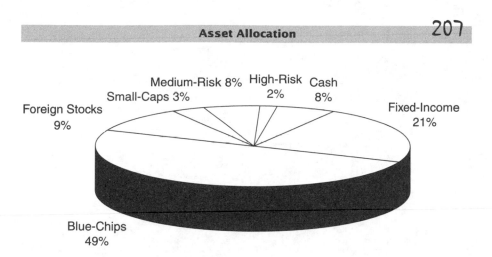

FIGURE 13.1 Sample target asset allocation based on ranges in Table 13.1.

tions as a benchmark or comparison tool for your current asset allocation. You may be assuming too much or too little risk based on your needs and circumstances.

If you are selecting fixed-income investments, you may want to select a mix of high-grade (investment-grade) corporate bonds and perhaps U.S. Treasury bonds or municipal bonds, depending on your income tax rate. It is often wise to invest in bonds that mature in 10 years or less.

Medium-risk assets may include utilities, real estate investment trusts (REITs), or other investment properties.

Your asset allocation may change depending on the stability and level of your income, the debt service payments you must make, the amount of money you need to support your family, and the time horizon for your objectives. For example, if you did not begin investing for retirement early in your working career, you may have to catch up and invest more money to make up for the shortfall and invest more aggressively to achieve the capital appreciation you need to enjoy your retirement.

Asset Allocation Pie Chart

The pie chart in Figure 13.1 represents only one combination of asset allocation. You may choose an entirely different asset allocation based on your needs and objectives.

Chapter 14

Retired People

PROFILE

This group includes people who may be married, divorced, or widowed, and who are in retirement or are planning to retire within a relatively short period of time. A member of this group typically:

- ✔ Is 55+ years old.
- ✔ Has an extended family where the children have graduated from college.
- ✔ Has reached peak earning years.
- ✔ Is planning a lifestyle for retirement.
- ✔ Is analyzing portfolio: assets, success, and future needs.
- ✔ Is determining the mix of income-producing assets and capital appreciation.
- ✔ Is adjusting their financial plan and investment program.
- ✔ Is facing changing spending patterns and household expenses due to retiring—forfeiting a salary or other type of earned income.
- ✔ Is deciding when to retire.
- ✔ Is deciding whether to postpone retirement in order to allow retirement plan assets to continue to grow.
- ✔ Is deciding whether to embark on a second career or part-time career in retirement.

✔ Is analyzing whether both spouses will retire at the same time.

✔ Rents or owns an apartment or house.

✔ Possibly owns an a vacation home.

✔ Owns or leases two cars.

✔ Takes one or more vacations per year.

✔ Most likely has paid down the home mortgage debt.

✔ Is investing money for retirement.

✔ Is planning for long-term care.

✔ Is planning for postretirement medical expenses.

✔ Is allocating money for final expenses.

This stage of life is typically characterized by a married couple or a divorced or widowed person planning for the next stage of life, which is retirement.

FINANCIAL OBJECTIVES

✔ Establishing a lifestyle that takes into account the likely retirement income level of the retiree.

✔ Planning an asset allocation that ensures that you will have an acceptable balance of capital appreciation, relatively low risk, and relatively high stable current income.

✔ Planning retirement in conjunction with maximizing employee and retirement benefits.

✔ Timing retirement to optimize your Social Security benefits.

✔ Preserving your wealth to last for your entire retirement years.

✔ Making the transition from being a member of the workforce to becoming a retiree.

✔ Reducing your debt.

✔ Downsizing such as selling a second car, moving to a smaller house, selling a boat, or selling a vacation home.

✔ Deciding whether and how much money to donate to charity.

✔ Updating your will.

✔ Reexamining your insurance policies.

OPPORTUNITIES

✔ Maximize your investments in your final working years to boost your retirement investment assets.

✔ Accelerate investments to tax-advantaged retirement programs.

✔ Continue to take advantage of compound returns.

✔ Rely on your pensions and Social Security payments for a year or two. Leave your retirement plan assets intact to grow tax-deferred for more time.

✔ Save money in advance to plan for increased costs and expenses.

✔ Plan for transition costs and expenses such as moving to a new home or retirement area.

✔ Review your lifestyle and fixed cost base to determine whether your spending levels are too high in light of your investment assets and other sources of retirement income and your desire to live a comfortable retirement.

✔ Choose a place to live if you intend to move to another area.

✔ Continue to become an educated consumer of financial products.

✔ Focus on how you can adjust your financial plan and portfolio to take advantage of income tax benefits and incentives and retirement plan distributions.

✔ Arrange your finances and retirement plan distributions to minimize your income taxes and penalties. There are typically penalties for making withdrawals from your retirement plans before you reach $59\frac{1}{2}$ years old and you must begin making withdrawals when you reach $70\frac{1}{2}$. Consult your tax adviser and financial planner to plan accordingly.

✔ Arrange your finances to minimize estate taxes.

✔ Learn how to manage your money in light of your fixed income and your inability to recover from major financial losses.

✔ Balance spending, saving, and investing.

✔ Analyze each spouse's financial opportunities—for example, when to utilize and how to maintain employee benefits such as retirement plans, insurance programs, and health insurance.

✔ Continue to reduce or eliminate debt, especially the home mortgage.

✔ Manage your spending carefully, especially since you no longer have a salary to replenish your investment portfolio.

✔ Avoid credit card debt.

✔ Pay off your credit card debt before it multiplies and you begin to rely on your investment portfolio to service credit card debt. This will impair the earning power of your investment portfolio.

✔ Manage your investments to provide a steady and perhaps increasing income over your retirement lifetime.

✔ Remember that typically you can assume the smallest degree of risk when you are retired because you have little ability to recover from major financial losses.

✔ Set aside money to fund long-term medical care and medical costs.

✔ Decide whether you want to execute a health care proxy and living will. Meet with your attorney and medical advisers.

✔ Give money to your children and grandchildren.

RISKS

✔ Failing to form a financial plan.

✔ Failing to implement your financial plan.

✔ Spending too much money.

✔ Not planning for increased expenses relating to inflation, a more active and expensive retirement lifestyle, and increasing and perhaps unforeseen medical costs.

✔ Being unrealistic about how much you can spend in retirement.

✔ Continuing to incur fixed costs at an unmanageable level.

✔ Continuing to incur consumer debt.

✔ Failing to save and invest enough money to continue to grow your portfolio to fund your income during the latter years of your retirement.

✔ Thinking you will spend a lot of money in your early retirement years and you will trim your spending and lifestyle later on. This is often unrealistic, especially in light of increasing costs, especially medical costs.

✔ Failing to establish a new financial plan in light of your revised goals, objectives, and financial circumstances.

✔ Carrying too much insurance or insurance that you don't need.

✔ Failing to update your will and estate plan.

One risk today is that once you retire you might have to care for and support your children and perhaps your parents. This is often called the "sandwich generation"—you are between two generations. You are providing financial support to your children and your parents at the same time. Today, many college graduates move back into their parents' home after graduation. Perhaps they need time to get established in their career or they need extra money to service student loans. This situation becomes particularly complex from a financial standpoint. Depending on how much assets the older generation has, this can put an enormous strain on your own finances and financial position. Plan accordingly and seek professional financial help as early as possible.

Another risk you may face is planning for and funding elder or long-term care. Unfortunately, many companies have curtailed or eliminated postretirement medical benefits. Former employees are now responsible for funding a higher percentage of their medical costs and expenses once they retire. Again, plan accordingly and seek professional financial advice early.

TIME HORIZON AND PLANNING

The time horizon for this group is surprisingly long—hopefully 25 to 35 years or so. At this point in your lives, it should be clear how much money you will have available to spend in retirement. You should have a clear understanding of the value of your investments and their potential for capital appreciation and the level of current income they can generate. You should also have a firm sense of how much in current income benefits you will collect during retirement such as annuity payments, pension payments, and Social Security payments. Just as you established a budget and spending plan during your earlier life stages, you must establish a similar plan once you retire.

Depending on where you are today in relation to achieving your financial goals and objectives, you may want to change your current lifestyle in order to maximize the likelihood you will achieve your long-range goals, especially living a comfortable retirement. You may want to defer your retirement for one, two, or three years. This will preserve your investment portfolio and hopefully enable it to grow now to provide additional income throughout your retirement years.

Meet with your tax adviser and financial planner to minimize the income tax consequences relating to withdrawing money from your retirement plans. For example, there are penalties associated with making withdrawals before you reach age $59\frac{1}{2}$ and you must begin making withdrawals when you reach $70\frac{1}{2}$. Also, depending on the state in which you live, you may be able to structure your investments and your pension plans to minimize your income tax burden.

Review your insurance policies. Cancel overlapping coverage. Suppose you carry a disability insurance policy that replaces your income in the event you become unable to work. If you take early retirement at age 55, you would not need disability insurance and it is likely that you would become ineligible for such a policy. Consider canceling such duplicate or unnecessary coverage.

Consider whether you would like to give money to your children and grandchildren. Under current U.S. income tax laws, each person can give up to $10,000 per year to another person. Typically, children pay income taxes at a lower rate than their parents (depending on how much passive income they earn). And, you can increase these amounts if you pay money directly to schools and medical institutions. Consult your income tax adviser.

This stage in your life offers you the opportunity to enjoy all your planning and financial success. If you are fortunate to have accumulated significant wealth and adequate sources of retirement income, you should enjoy your retirement years. However, it is difficult to gauge your actual lifespan, how your investment portfolio will perform, how much money you will actually spend in retirement, and how much your cost of living will rise.

The authors have counseled people who accumulated significant investment portfolios and underestimated their likely financial needs in retirement and the amount one needs to invest to build enough wealth to fund the desired retirement lifestyle. Many people establish a lifestyle and a fixed cost base that consumes more of their portfolio income and principal than they would ideally like. This often means that you will reduce your earning assets at a faster rate than you want. This could result in your depleting your portfolio and being short of funds. If your analysis shows that you may outlive your investment assets, you may want to take this opportunity to trim your expenses and reinvest dividends and other distributions to increase the value and earning power of your investments.

Asset allocation is important at this life stage as well as in earlier stages. Even if you are 50 or 60 years old, it is likely that you will live for another 25 to 35 years. This means that you still need to grow your portfolio, and capital appreciation is an important component of your financial well-being. The younger you are and the longer your time horizon, the more important it is to consider investing a greater percentage of your money in common stocks and other assets that have the potential to appreciate in value and serve as a potential hedge against inflation. This is important, especially if you hope to live in retirement for at least 25 or 35 years.

While people's income tends to rise over time, their costs and expenses tend to rise over time as well. If you analyze your personal life horizon and plan accordingly, you can spend your current pension and Social Security income and reinvest your distributions to build your investment portfolio today, especially if you have not invested enough money in the past. This way, you can still take advantage of compound returns and income tax deferral. You still can build some additional wealth for retirement, although not as much as in earlier life stages. As you get older, it becomes more and more important to adopt a more conservative stance and take action to build enough wealth for retirement.

As a member of this group, you are likely to face various financial needs, including funding some or all of your children's and parents' living expenses, perhaps servicing credit card debt, and funding long-term care. It is worthwhile to balance your retirement lifestyle and your spending. For example, it would be wise to put yourself on a relatively conservative spending plan, especially in the early years of your retirement, and leave your investments intact to grow to provide greater income and spending dollars during your latter retirement years. Reexamine and monitor your employee benefits and in particular any distribution rules and restrictions regarding pensions, Social Security benefits, and postretirement medical benefits. You may want to continue working with your present company for several years before retiring, or you may decide to embark on a second career.

Downsize your lifestyle as much as practical to reduce your ongoing expenses. Pay down as much debt as possible to reduce your fixed obligations and your interest expense.

It is also helpful to segregate your money into different pools to achieve specific objectives. It is likely that you will want to channel a por-tion of your income to fund your leisure activities such as travel and en-tertainment and to fuel your investment portfolios. The key is to assess your financial goals and plan your life and your finances accordingly.

INVESTMENT OPPORTUNITIES

✔ Investing in assets that have a relatively high probability to grow (capital appreciation). You should emphasize higher-quality and more reliable assets that pay consistent dividends and other dis-tributions and still offer reasonable growth potential.

✔ Increasing the percentage of your portfolio that provides current and stable income. One way to accomplish this goal is to invest in a blue-chip common stock mutual fund or a mutual fund that in-vests primarily in common stocks that have a long-standing his-tory of paying quarterly dividends and raising their dividends.

✔ Trimming your living and discretionary expenses so that you can manage your investment portfolio to fund your income through-out your retirement years.

✔ Splitting your portfolio into two components: one for current in-come and one for continued capital appreciation.

✔ Determining how much, if any, of your principal you will spend and when. Once you begin depleting the principal portion of your in-vestment portfolio, you surrender the investments' earning power, and this means you will probably have lower income later on.

Consider investing some money in a high-quality blue-chip common stock mutual fund, equity income fund, or closed-end mutual fund that has a top track record and pays a relatively high dividend.

Closed-end mutual funds trade on the New York Stock Exchange or other stock exchanges. Closed-end mutual funds have mixed track records, especially compared to many of the S&P 500 Index mutual funds. However, closed-end mutual funds that pay a relatively high an-nual dividend offer both capital appreciation and a base for your portfolio and wealth building program. The shares of a closed-end mutual fund trade at a premium or discount to the value of the securities owned by the portfolio. Suppose a closed-end mutual fund trades at $10 per share on the New York Stock Exchange and the net asset value of the portfolio equals $12 per share. This fund trades at a 16.67 percent discount to net asset value. Consider funds that trade at a relatively steep discount to their net asset value and that are at a relative low to their historic discount. If you invest in a closed-end mutual fund, reinvest your distributions and purchase additional shares in the fund.

As you advance to this life stage and in the future, you should commit none of your money to relatively risky asset categories because you have little power to recover from major financial losses. Focus more on assets that offer capital appreciation and pay current dividends.

INVESTMENT RISKS

- ✔ Not considering each spouse's objectives, investment style, and risk tolerance.
- ✔ Not continuing to invest in assets that offer capital appreciation.
- ✔ Not controlling your costs and expenses.
- ✔ Not investing aggressively enough to meet your retirement needs.
- ✔ Spending too much of your investment income in the early years of your retirement.
- ✔ Spending too much of your investment principal in the early years of your retirement.
- ✔ Investing too much money in low-yielding assets such as money market instruments, certificates of deposit, and U.S. Treasury securities.
- ✔ Investing money in high-risk assets such as options, futures, venture capital, and other hit-or-miss investments.
- ✔ Not updating your will.

ASSET ALLOCATION

Table 14.1 and Figure 14.1 present a range of target asset allocations—the percentage of your money that you might want to allocate to each investment category. It is crucial that you consider these target percentages

TABLE 14.1 Sample Target Asset Allocation Percentages for Retirees	
Asset Category	*Allocation Percentages*
Cash and equivalents	0 to 20
Fixed-income investments	25 to 50
Blue-chip common stocks	35 to 50
Foreign blue-chip common stocks	5 to 10
Small-capitalization common stocks	0
Medium-risk assets not covered above	5 to 10
High-risk assets	0

Note: The target percentages add up to more or less than 100 percent at each end of the ranges because different people are likely to allocate their money in different ways across asset categories.

as a sample illustration and you consider them in light of your own personal objectives and circumstances. Be sure to consult with your financial professionals and advisers. At the very least, use these allocations as a benchmark or comparison tool for your current asset allocation. You may be assuming too much or too little risk based on your needs and circumstances.

If you are selecting fixed-income investments, you may want to select a mix of high-grade (investment-grade) corporate bonds and perhaps U.S. Treasury bonds or municipal bonds, depending on your income tax rate. It is often wise to invest in bonds that mature in 10 years or less.

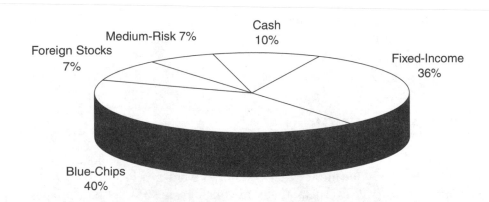

FIGURE 14.1 Sample target asset allocation based on ranges in Table 14.1.

Medium-risk assets may include utilities, real estate investment trusts (REITs), or other investment properties.

Your asset allocation may change depending on the stability and level of your income, the debt service payments you must make, the amount of money you need to support your family, and the time horizon for your objectives. For example, the lower your pension and Social Security benefits and the higher your standard of living, the more money you will need from your investment portfolio. This has a direct result on the amount of your investment assets and the level of compound growth and appreciation they can achieve over the long run.

Asset Allocation Pie Chart

The pie chart in Figure 14.1 represents only one combination of asset allocation. You may choose an entirely different asset allocation based on your needs and objectives.

Chapter

Maximizing Wealth through Asset Allocation

This chapter ties together the asset allocation techniques described in Chapter 4 and the profiles covered in Chapters 10 through 14. It is designed to help you implement an asset allocation program on a long-term basis and maximize your wealth.

SIMPLE VERSUS COMPLEX

Now that you have read this book, you can see that asset allocation is relatively straightforward. It is relatively simple in that it is the first step in the implementation of your financial plan. However, it can be relatively complex in that one size does not fit all. Despite the fact that financial planners and brokerage houses recommend model portfolios—in effect, asset allocations—your personal circumstances and financial position are likely to be different from the next person's financial position. Therefore, it is important for you to establish your own personal asset allocation.

STRIKE A BALANCE

Utilize the model portfolios that appear in Chapters 10 through 14 and compare those target asset allocations to your current asset allocation and your financial planner's or brokerage house model portfolio. Your invest-ment results will be largely the result of two factors: the return on your in-vestments and the weightings in each asset class.

For example, according to Ibbotson Associates, Inc., in 1997 the S&P 500 index returned 33.36 percent and long-term corporate bonds re-turned 12.95 percent. (Used with permission. © 1998 Ibbotson Associ-ates, Inc. All rights reserved.) Table 15.1 shows the expected returns based on several model portfolios.

Once you establish a reasonable asset allocation for yourself, you can begin selecting investments that will help you achieve your financial and personal goals.

PERIODIC REVIEW

Asset allocation, like all other systems and plans, requires periodic and regular monitoring. After all, your financial future is at stake here. We rec-ommend that investors review their portfolios and asset allocations:

✔ At least once per year.

✔ After you file your income tax return.

✔ When you receive a windfall.

✔ When the securities markets move more than 10 percent to 15 percent, up or down.

✔ When your personal circumstances change.

✔ When you get closer to your target date for realizing your goals.

TABLE 15.1 Sample Asset Allocation and Blended Rate of Return			
Portfolio	Percent Invested in Common Stocks	Percent Invested in Bonds	Approximate Blended Return
I	100%	0%	11.0%
II	75	25	9.6
III	50	50	8.25
IV	25	75	6.9
V	0	100	5.5

TIME CHANGES ALL

People say, "Time heals all." And to some extent this is true, especially over the long run given compound returns. However, you and your financial circumstances will change over time, and the relative values of the asset classes and hence your asset allocation are likely to change over time.

REBALANCING YOUR PORTFOLIO

Rebalancing your portfolio means adjusting your investments to bring your portfolio back into line with your target asset allocation. When you complete this task once per year, you are at least halfway there regarding becoming a successful investor. This is because the key to successful investing is discipline. By establishing an investment program based on your specific and personal asset allocation, you are becoming a disciplined investor.

Suppose your target asset allocation is 60 percent common stocks and 40 percent bonds. At the beginning of the year, you allocate your $100,000 investment portfolio as in Table 15.2.

On January 2 of the next year, you review your portfolio and you are pleased to learn that the common stocks returned 11 percent and the bonds returned 6 percent. Your portfolio would now be worth $109,000 (See Table 15.3).

TABLE 15.2 Example of Asset Allocation		
Investment	*Allocation*	*Value*
Common stocks	60%	$ 60,000
Bonds	40	40,000
Totals	100%	$100,000

TABLE 15.3 Asset Value Breakdown at End of first Year				
Investment	*Beginning Value*	*Rate of Return*	*Return*	*Ending Value*
Common stocks	$ 60,000	11%	$6,600	$ 66,000
Bonds	40,000	6%	2,400	42,400
Totals	$100,000		$9,000	$109,000

Overall, your return was 9 percent; or, $109,000 ending value minus $100,000 beginning value equals $9,000 divided by $100,000 equals 9 percent. Another way to calculate your overall return is on a weighted average basis, shown in Table 15.4. If 60 percent of your portfolio earned 11 percent (a percentage return of 6.6 percent), and 40 percent of your portfolio earned 6 percent (a percentage return of 2.4 percent), then the weighted average return would equal 9 percent (the sum of 6.6 percent and 2.4 percent).

The first step to rebalance your portfolio is to calculate the actual allocation of your investment portfolio. (See Table 15.5.) In our example, the portfolio value rose from $100,000 to $109,000. The value of the common stocks equals $66,600 and the bonds $42,400. Now common stocks represent 61.1 percent of the portfolio and bonds 38.9 percent. (This example assumes that your entire portfolio consists of only these two assets. If you held other assets and investments, your calculation would be more complex.)

Next, it is important to decide whether you should change your target asset allocation. As we illustrated in the model portfolios in Chapters 10 through 14, your target asset allocation is likely to change over time.

Suppose you decide to hold your target asset allocation constant. In our example, that would mean adjusting your investment portfolio such that common stocks represented the original 60 percent of your portfolio and bonds 40 percent. Currently, common stocks comprise 61.1 percent of the portfolio. Therefore, we need to move 1.1 percent of

TABLE 15.4 Weighted Average Return on Portfolio			
Investment	Allocation	Return	Weighted Average
Common Stocks	60%	11%	6.6%
Bonds	40	6	2.4
Totals	100%		9.0%

TABLE 15.5 Calculating Actual Asset Allocation			
Investment	Value	Total Portfolio Value	Allocation
Common stocks	$ 66,600	$109,000	61.1%
Bonds	42,400	109,000	38.9
Totals	$109,000		100.0%

the total portfolio value from common stocks to bonds, or other asset classes as appropriate.

To calculate how much money to move, you would find 1.1 percent of the total portfolio value of $109,000, or $1,199. Table 15.6 illustrates how to calculate how much money to move from common stocks to bonds in this sample asset allocation.

Another way to calculate these amounts is to calculate the target amounts or values of each desired investment class based on the current value of your portfolio as of the valuation date. For example, if you wanted to maintain 60 percent of your portfolio in common stocks and your portfolio value equaled $109,000, you would want to invest $65,400 in common stocks. Since the current value of your common stocks equals $66,600, you would want to move $1,199 to another asset class.

To maintain your target asset allocation, you would sell $1,199 or $1,200 (rounded) of common stocks and invest that same amount in bonds. Now your asset allocation would be 60 percent common stocks and 40 percent bonds. Table 15.7 illustrates how much money to move between one investment class and another, in this case common stocks to bonds. Table 15.8 shows your asset allocation after you adjust your portfolio to return to your target asset allocation.

TABLE 15.6   Calculating Move from Common Stocks to Bonds

Allocation	Common Stocks
Current allocation amount	61.1%
Target percentage allocation	60%
Difference	1.1%
Portfolio value	$109,000
Required adjustment	$1,199

TABLE 15.7   Calculating Move from One Investment Class to Another

Investment	Beginning Value	Adjustment	Ending Value
Common stocks	$ 66,600	($1,200)	$ 65,400
Bonds	42,400	1,200	43,600
Totals	$109,000	0	$109,000

TABLE 15.8 Adjusted Asset Allocation		
Investment	Allocation	Value
Common stocks	60%	$ 65,400
Bonds	40	43,600
Totals	100%	$109,000

VALUE APPROACH

The theory behind this disciplined exercise is that you are pursuing a value strategy, believing that over the long term, asset returns follow their historical rates of return. This may or may not be accurate, because major shifts in economics and politics may mean that the future will not repeat the past. Under this model, the theory is that if stocks outperform bonds, you would want to realize some of the profits you earned on common stocks and channel them to bonds. Your assumption is that bonds would revert to their historic rates of return. This approach helps you to manage your asset allocation and avoid an overconcentration of assets in any one particular asset class and avoid market timing.

ASSET ALLOCATION AND SUBCATEGORIES

The examples in this chapter assume that you invest your money in only common stocks and bonds. This is an unrealistic assumption. If you pursue a typical asset allocation, you would want to channel your investments across a number of investments including low-risk, medium-risk, and high-risk assets. Further, you would not want your portfolio to have a relatively high concentration or overweighting in any one asset class. The most effective way to calculate your asset allocation is to multiply your target asset allocation for each investment category by your total portfolio value on the valuation date, as just discussed. This tactic would help you allocate your money to each of your desired investment categories.

DECIDING WHICH ASSETS TO SELL

Often, it is relatively easy to determine an asset allocation on paper. But in reality, executing your strategy can be relatively complicated. Here are a number of factors to consider when you adjust your investment portfolio to achieve your target asset allocation:

✔ Sell those investments in your retirement plan accounts where there should be no income tax consequences related to their liquidation.

✔ Consider the investment choices offered in your retirement plan. With many employer-sponsored retirement plans, there are only 6 to 10 investment options. When you liquidate some of your holdings in your retirement plan account, the other options offered may not be attractive.

✔ Before selling an investment, review its performance against the performance of its peer group. In other words, if you own a common stock mutual fund and are considering selling your mutual fund shares, how has that mutual fund performed compared to other mutual funds with the same investment objective?

✔ Consider moving funds within the same mutual fund family to simplify recordkeeping and minimize your transaction costs. Nonetheless, investment performance should be your overriding concern.

✔ If you hold tax-advantaged debt in your retirement plan account, you should sell those investments as soon as practical. This includes municipal bonds and U.S. Treasury securities. Since the interest income on these securities is already exempt from income taxes, there is no value to your holding these investments in a tax-deferred account that provides additional tax relief. One exception to this rule may be a zero coupon U.S. Treasury bond where the interest income is taxable to you in the year you accrue the interest and you receive no cash interest coupon payments.

✔ Consider holding your foreign mutual funds in a regular account and not a retirement plan account. Often, mutual funds that invest in securities of companies based in foreign countries pay dividends and interest that are subject to foreign taxes. Under current U.S. tax law, in general you would be entitled to a tax credit equal to the amount of the foreign tax you paid. When you hold these investments in a retirement plan, you lose the value of the tax credit.

✔ Consider holding your retirement plan assets constant, with the exception of rebalancing your investments to meet your asset allocation. For most people, the retirement plan assets represent long-term money and very important money. Frequent trading often results in reducing your overall investment returns.

✔ If your investments are performing in line with their peers and the overall securities markets, consider leaving your current asset allocation intact and channel new money toward those categories you want to increase.

✔ If in doubt, conduct more research and engage a financial professional to help you position your assets wisely.

For asset allocation to be effective, you must develop and implement a long-term and consistent program. The key to success is sound financial analysis and discipline.

Epilogue

Looking to the Future

Asset allocation is a powerful investment discipline. While asset allocation cannot select specific investments for you, asset allocation can help you select types of investments and asset classes that will help you implement your financial plan. The key to financial success is discipline. It is crucial to adopt a sound long-term strategy and follow the plan. Many investors fall prey to emotion and psychology and invest their money accordingly. By determining an asset allocation for you, you can create a point-by-point strategy for the long term.

Here are five key action steps to follow:

1. Establish financial goals and objectives. The key to making any plan begins with selecting one or more specific targets. And set milestones—times when you want to reach certain goals and yardsticks to measure or track your progress and results.

2. Determine a financial plan that is designed to help you achieve your goals and objectives.

3. Establish an asset allocation that will help you divide your investment capital into the appropriate asset classes to mesh with your financial plan.

4. Select the best or optimal investments in each asset class and implement an asset allocation.

5. Monitor your results. At least once every year, review your portfolio. Compare your actual returns, and update your asset allocation against your target asset allocation. Make changes to your portfolio in light of your actual rates of return and your

target asset allocation. Change your investments and your asset allocation as your goals, objectives, and circumstances change over time.

The key to a successful financial plan is *you*—your goals and objectives, your financial position, and your personal circumstances. Become an educated consumer of financial products and make a financial plan. Then implement your plan and asset allocation.

Glossary

actuals   trading in the commodity itself; at the end of the life of a futures contract, the owner actually receives or takes delivery of the gold, silver, soybeans, and so on.

agency securities   securities issued by an agency of the federal government such as the Federal National Mortgage Association or the Government National Mortgage Association. Such securities may or may not be direct obligations of the federal government, since it is the agency of the government rather than the government (the people) borrowing the money.

American depositary receipts (ADRs)   negotiable receipts traded in the United States that represent shares of a foreign company. These shares are held in trust by a trustee (typically a bank) for the benefit of the U.S. investor, who is entitled to receive all dividends and capital gains distributions from the foreign shares.

American depositary shares (ADSs)   typically used interchangeably with ADRs, but the company that issued the stock rather than the trustee holds the ADSs.

annual report   a report issued once per year by a company's senior management that contains the company's financial statements, management's letter, information about the company, and often glossy photos of the company's operations.

annuity   a payment stream over a period of time, usually from an insurance company.

ask   the price at which you can buy an investment from the market maker.

asset allocation   division of assets to accomplish personal goals based on age, financial time horizons, financial position, personal risk tolerance, family needs, years to retirement, and so on.

assets   things/property owned. Your assets would include your home, car, stocks, bonds, collectibles, and so on, while your business might own machinery, equipment, and land.

balance sheet   statement of financial condition: assets owned, liabilities owed, and the shareholders' equity.

bankable   from the standpoint of film deals, a bankable star or personality would be one who has successfully drawn a crowd to previous films, made money over the years for various movie companies by appearing in their films, and whose name, when associated with a new film project, lends a comfort level to the people financing the deal. The bankable star's participation acts as a form of collateral for the investors.

bid   the price at which an investor can sell an investment to the market maker.

board of directors   group of professionals who govern a corporation or other organization, typically comprised of leaders in industry and top executives of the company. Shareholders vote to approve the election of directors.

bonds   evidence of an obligation to repay in the form of promissory notes or IOUs usually issued by a corporation, municipality, government or government agency to the holder. Bonds usually run for 10 or more years to maturity.

bullion   the actual gold, silver, or platinum metal, typically in bar form, traded based on the actual value of the metal without numismatic considerations. Bullion coins are traded based on the value of the metal irrespective of collectible considerations or history.

call   a type of option giving the owner the right to purchase a security from the grantor (the seller of the option) at a fixed price (the exercise price) for a predetermined period of time. Calls are usually purchased in anticipation of a rising market.

capital appreciation   the increase in the value of an investment held and not yet sold.

cash value   the dollars built up in an insurance policy from dividends earned or investments made by the issuer. Cash value can be borrowed from yourself and has the effect of lowering the death benefit on the policy. The older the policy, the greater the amount of cash value available. Term insurance doesn't build cash value, but just provides coverage.

certificate of deposit (CD)   loan made by an individual to a bank.

commission   fee charged by one person/entity to act on behalf of another. Your broker charges you a commission to execute a trade, just as the real estate agent charges you a commission when you buy a house.

commodities   the physical assets, including meats, orange juice, metals, including gold and silver.

convertible   a security that can be changed into another security—for example, a convertible bond or convertible preferred stock that can be exchanged for shares of the company's common stock.

correlation   the relationship between two or more different securities held in a portfolio where one rises in value when the other falls or one goes up in value and the other goes up as well. A well-balanced portfolio would have assets allocated to make this happen during active markets.

coupon   piece of paper attached to a bond that represents the semiannual interest due to the bondholder. A typical 30-year coupon bond would have 60 coupons representing the semiannual interest payments for the next 30 years or the remaining life of the bond. When the coupon is detached and sent to the bank named, the bondholder receives a check for six months of the interest due.

covered call   an investor holds 100 shares of common stock and sells a call. The call option is said to be covered because the writer of the call option owns shares of the underlying common stock.

cumulative preferred   a share of preferred stock where the company must pay all dividends due on preferred stock before declaring any dividends to the common stockholders and owes you the arrears.

defined-benefit plans   the payout or pension benefit is defined in dollars.

defined-contribution plans   the company contributes a specific or defined amount of money into your pension account today and you are responsible for managing your own money.

derivatives   securities that are created using other securities or parts thereof. They derive their value from the success or failure of the underlying security and not from sales, profits, or other activities. Examples are DIAMONDS and "spiders," basically trusts whose value is based on the rise and fall of the value of the 30 components of the Dow Jones Industrial Average and the S&P 500 Index, respectively.

dilution   literally, "watering down" the value of shares by a subsequent recapitalization of a company. Example of dilution of ownership: You own 100 shares of a company with 1000 shares issued and outstanding. At this point you hold 10 percent of the shares. The company issues and sells another 1000 shares to the general public. Now you own 100 out of 2000 shares, or 5 percent.

discount   purchase of a bond at an amount that is less than the face value or redemption value. A bond purchased at $95^3/_4$ is bought at 95.75 percent of the face value or redemption value of $1000 or $957.50. Such a discounted purchase would mean the bondholder would receive a higher yield than if bought at face value.

discount rate   the rate of interest the Federal Reserve Bank charges member banks to borrow against their own reserves. An increase in the discount rate is said to signal a period of tight money, and a drop in the discount rate by the Fed would indicate easy money. Such moves are usually followed by an increase or drop in the member banks' lending rates.

diversification   spreading your assets among different securities (growth, income, etc.) or different quality securities within an asset class or mutual fund for the purpose of spreading out your risk. The opposite of diversification would be having all your eggs in one basket.

dividend   payout by a corporation to its preferred and common shareholders of moneys from earnings. Dividend payments usually occur on a quarterly or semiannual basis out of already taxed dollars.

dividend reinvestment plan (DRIP)   a program where holders of shares of common stock can elect to reinvest their quarterly dividends in additional shares of the common stock, sometimes at a discount.

dividend yield   the annual dividend payout in dollars divided by the current market value of the common stock ($1 annual dividend divided by $25 market price equals 4 percent dividend yield).

earnings per share (EPS)   a company's accounting earnings for the last period (quarter or year) divided by the weighted average number of shares outstanding for the period.

earnings yield the inverse of price-earnings or P/E ratio. The market value of the common stock divided by the last four quarters' or years' earnings.

equipment leasing transactions similar to real estate rental property; an owner buys equipment and rents it to a user.

equity stock representing ownership rather than a bond representing a debt owed by the corporation to the bondholders. Equity is also the difference between the value of something owned and the debt owed against it. If you own a $250,000 home with a $150,000 mortgage, your equity in that asset is the difference, or $100,000.

exercise the holder of a put or call option can choose to exercise the option. In the case of a call option, the holder calls the stock away from the writer and buys the shares of the common stock at the option strike price. In the case of a put option, the holder puts the stock to the writer and sells the shares of common stock at the option strike price.

exercise price in the world of options, the fixed price the owner of an option has the right to pay to (for a call) or demand from (for a put) the seller or grantor for the underlying stock over the life of the option. Same as the strike price.

fixed annuity pays a (minimum) fixed rate of return, and represents a credit obligation of the party (usually an insurance company) promising to make the annuity payment stream.

fixed income the semiannual interest paid by a government or corporation to its bondholders. This amount, expressed in dollars, remains fixed even if the market price of the bond fluctuates in response to market conditions.

float the number of shares issued by a corporation that is in the hands of the shareholders as opposed to the total number of shares that that entity could otherwise ultimately issue (sometimes referred to as the public float); the outstanding and tradable shares. In the banking community the term applies to the time period between the writing of a check and its actual clearing at the bank upon which it was written.

foreign bonds fixed-income securities issued by governments of foreign countries and by companies based in countries outside the United States.

full faith and credit usually applies to the bond or debt market and means that no specific asset stands behind that debt, but rather the borrower's full faith and credit. In the world of government debt that backing represents the government's ability to print money (tax the people).

futures   the trading in commodities such as grains, orange juice, metals, and even interest rates.

gain   the amount of money by which the market value of a security exceeds the purchase price of that security. If you purchased a share of ABC Company common stock for $43 and today the market value of that stock is $52, your gain would equal $9.

general obligation (G.O.) bonds   obligations backed by the borrower's full faith and credit. General obligation municipal bonds are those backed by the issuer's taxing authority, as opposed to revenue bonds, which depend on the revenues generated by the project financed, like a toll road or a bridge.

governments   U.S. government obligations, including Treasury bills, Treasury notes, Treasury bonds, and the debt of various U.S. government agencies (agency securities).

grantor   in the world of options, the seller of an option and the one who stands ready either to sell the underlying stock in the case of granting a call option or to buy the underlying stock back in the case of the grantor of a put option.

hedge   a strategy employed when you want to offset one or more types of investment risk using another investment vehicle. You feel that the market price of a particular stock you own may go down in the future and you want to protect those gains already realized. You could purchase a put option and lock in the price at which you could sell (put the stock to the grantor of that option) during the next three months.

index   a measurement of change. The Dow Jones Industrial Average measures the fluctuation of the 30 components that make up that index. There are indexes for the New York Stock Exchange, the American Stock Exchange, the Standard & Poor's 500, and the Value Line, just to name a few.

indexed   the tying of taxes, wages, and so on to one or more of the broad indexes followed by economists so they would rise or fall with the index.

inflation   the loss of purchasing power due to increased prices. As the prices of food, fuel, and housing rise, more dollars are required to purchase those goods and services.

initial public offering (IPO)   when the company or its investment bankers sell shares of the company's common stock to the public (individual investors) or mutual funds for the first time.

interest   paid to the lender by the borrower, this is the cost of using money. The most common form of interest is the amount you pay the bank to borrow the money used to purchase your house. This is known as mortgage interest and is generally paid on a monthly basis along with a part of the principal. If you lend money to a corporation or government by buying their bonds, they pay you a semiannual amount for the use of that money and then repay the principal upon the maturity of that bond, frequently as long as 20 or 30 years out.

intrinsic value   the value of that which makes up what you own. The intrinsic value of a gold coin would be the current market price of gold times the weight of the coin in question. In the world of options, the intrinsic value of the option would be the difference between the market price of the stock and the strike price. If you own a call with a strike price of $45 and the stock is selling at $47, the intrinsic value of the option is $2. Out-of-the-money options and options trading at-the-money have no intrinsic value.

investment-grade bonds   bonds rated among the top four categories by the major rating services.

junk bonds   bonds issued by companies with either a very short financial track record or a very poor credit rating and credit history. Having a Standard & Poor's or Moody's credit rating of BB+ or lower, they would not be considered investment-grade.

ladder   staggering the maturities of debt instruments to obtain an average return (e.g., investing $100,000 in U.S. Treasury bonds by buying $20,000 pieces maturing at, say, two-year intervals going forward).

large-cap (large-capitalization) stock   stock of a company where the market value of all of its common stock that is issued and outstanding exceeds $5 billion (this number is a market convention and may change over time).

leverage   the use of debt to purchase something more expensive than you could otherwise afford to buy for all cash. The most common form of leverage is the purchase of a home. For example, the house costs $250,000, but all you have in cash is $100,000. You accomplish the purchase with a mortgage of $150,000 leveraging your cash to acquire a

$250,000 asset. The higher the degree of leverage, the greater the percentage of return on (or loss of) your money.

limit order   an order to buy or sell a security at a specific price. Once the market price hits the limit, the trade would be executed as long as there is no stock ahead of you.

loads   fees or sales commissions paid for the purchase of mutual funds. Generally, the traditional load or sales charge to purchase a mutual fund is 8.5 percent of the purchase price. A load of less than 8.5 percent indicates a low-load fund; in some cases there is no up-front sales charge, and we have what is known as a no-load fund. Also known as the sales charge or the commission.

loss   the amount by which the market value of a security has declined below the price at which you purchased it. If you purchased one share of ABC Company common stock at $26 and the current market value equals $16, your loss equals $10.

margin   money borrowed to purchased securities.

margin requirements   also known as margin rate; the amount you can borrow from the brokerage house to purchase securities. The current margin rate is 50 percent of the purchase price on applicable stocks. When the Federal Reserve Board raises the requirement it is tightening money, and when it lowers the requirement it is easing the money supply.

market maker   a broker-dealer firm that buys and sells securities for its own account. This firm stands ready to buy securities (make a bid) and sell securities (make an offer) in particular companies they either like or may have been active in bringing public. This activity is performed by a specialist on the floors of the various exchanges.

market timing   using various indexes that measure the state of the economy, interest rates, or other variables to make buy and sell decisions (e.g., you expect interest rates to drop because of certain seasonal factors, etc., so you purchase fixed-income securities whose value will rise as interest rates fall).

market value   the current value of a security. If you owned a share of ABC Company common stock and the bid price of the stock was $72, you could sell that share of stock for $72 minus sales commissions.

maturity   the date the face amount of a debt security comes due and must be paid by the borrower. At maturity, the holder of a bond is owed the full face value of that bond regardless of market conditions. Some debt instruments mature in 10, 20, or even 30 years from their date of issue.

money market certificates represent participation in a portfolio of money market instruments at a bank or other financial institution.

money market instruments short-term securities or deposits that mature within a period of 270 days to one year.

money market mutual fund a mutual fund that invests in money market instruments.

money market securities have a short term to maturity, generally 270 days or less are extremely liquid, and carry relatively low risk.

mortgage the amount of money borrowed to purchase a home. Sometimes, the money borrowed (margined) to purchase securities; a first mortgage bond would be one backed by a lien on a specific piece of real property owned by the borrower/issuer.

municipal bonds (munis) bonds issued by cities, communities, towns, or other political entities (in effect, moneys borrowed by the people of the community) for projects related to that community. Munis are often used to finance schools, hospitals, toll roads, tunnels, sewers, or fire equipment, and the interest paid is free from federal taxation. If the muni is owned by a resident of the city that issued it, that resident's income from such a bond could be triple tax-free—exempt from federal, state, and city income taxes.

mutual fund pool of money managed by an investment professional.

National Association of Securities Dealers Automated Quotations system (NASDAQ) an exchangeless market because there is no physical exchange where stocks are traded. Brokers and dealers trade NASDAQ-listed securities directly with each other by phone or computer.

net asset value (NAV) the fair market value of the securities held by the mutual fund. NAV is often calculated as follows: fund's assets minus fund's liabilities divided by mutual fund shares.

no-risk investments since we are all going to suffer from buying power risk over time, the only type of investment that can be said to be riskless would be one that isn't marketable and isn't subject to market risk. United States savings bonds, passbook savings accounts (up to the insured limits of the bank), and bank certificates of deposit (again, up to the insured limits of the bank) are nonmarketable, and therefore riskless, investments you could make.

numismatic   relating to the study of or collection of coins. As opposed to intrinsic value (the value of the metal in said coin), a coin's numismatic value would be based on its population (how many were ever produced), its historic significance, and its condition.

options   the right or privilege (but not the obligation) to buy (for a call) or sell (for a put) something in the future.

paper profit   the unrealized difference between the purchase price of any investment and its current higher value. For example, you bought a stock a number of years ago and invested $5000; today that same stock is worth $10,000; you have an unrealized profit of $5000. Paper profits aren't taxable until and unless realized.

par   the face value of a bond, traditionally $1000.

payable date   the date on which a coupon or dividend is payable to an investor.

penny stock   any stock selling at $5 or less per share. Penny stocks are usually stocks of new companies with little or no financial history or trading track record and for the most part are for those investors with a high risk tolerance. Sometimes called cats and dogs.

population   in the world of coins and stamps, the number of a particular item that were at one time minted or printed. Pennies have been minted in the United States by the billions every year and have a huge population/low value. Postage stamps are usually printed by the hundred million. A stamp or coin with a low population would generally bespeak greater value. Silver coins whose populations have been reduced by being melted down for their intrinsic value when silver ran up above $40 per ounce are now worth more than before.

premium   the difference between the face value/maturity value of a bond and its higher current market value. A bond selling at $104^{1}/_{2}$ is selling at more than face value and is said to be at a premium of $4^{1}/_{2}$ points. Also, the price of an option.

price-earnings ratio (P/E)   reflection of the number times the earnings per share the stock is selling at. If a company shows earnings of $2.50 per share and the market price is $27^{1}/_{2}$, the stock is selling at a P/E of 11 or is worth 11 times the earnings of $2.50 per share. Historically a P/E of below

20 has been considered conservative and a P/E above 20 has been considered more speculative.

prospectus   a printed description of an enterprise that is distributed to prospective buyers; in the case of securities, a summary of the registration statement filed with the SEC that explains the nature of the security being offered to the public.

put   an option that allows the owner to sell the underlying security to the seller/grantor of the option at a fixed price for a fixed period of time. Puts are usually purchased in anticipation of a declining market to lock in as much of the current value as possible.

realized capital gain   a gain that has been taken—you sold an investment at a price higher than the price at which you acquired it.

realized gain   the difference between the purchase price and the higher selling price of a security that has been taken by selling the asset. A realized gain is a taxable event, as opposed to an unrealized gain or a paper profit.

record date   the date on which the investor in a common or preferred stock is entitled to receive the dividend declared by the board of directors. If the investor sells the common stock the day after the record date, the seller will still receive the dividend because they remain owners until the settlement date.

redeem   to turn in for payment at maturity. If you bought a bond a number of years ago and that bond matured this year, you would return the bond to the issuer for payment of the face value. Upon redemption, you could now reinvest the proceeds elsewhere.

retained earnings   after-tax accounting earnings held by the company for reinvestment. Typically companies pay a portion of their earnings to common stockholders in the form of dividends and retain the remainder.

return   reward on an investment. Return can be expressed in a number of ways in the world of money: the dividends received on a stock owned, interest on a bond, the satisfaction of stability in your portfolio, and a combination of dividends or interest with appreciation to produce total return.

revenue bond   a type of municipal bond that is backed by the revenue income from the project financed rather than the taxing authority of the issuer. Revenue bonds are frequently issued to pay for toll roads (backed by the tolls) and sewer installations (backed by sewer hookup charges).

reward the benefits you received in exchange for what you paid or what action you took. Perhaps you purchased shares of common stock and the price rose; your reward is the realized gain. Or, you bought a bond and received interest; your reward is the interest income.

risk the uncertainty or probability of achieving or not achieving a certain outcome or expected rate of return.

risk tolerance how much of anything owned you are prepared to lose. Can you tolerate the loss of 25 percent of your assets and still be able to feel comfortable? Or, are you a person who cannot bear to see $1 of your portfolio lost? Somewhere between that first dollar and all you have will be a true expression of your individual risk tolerance level. No two people have the same ability to tolerate risk.

sales charges fees charged to buy and sell mutual funds (aka loads).

securities and exchange commission (SEC) the U.S. governmental agency that governs the U.S. securities markets and the securities industry; established in 1934.

stock dividends dividends paid to shareholders in the form of additional shares of the company's stock rather than in cash. During its growth phase a company would want to conserve cash and use it to continue to expand. By paying dividends in the form of shares instead of cash, it can accomplish both goals.

stock option not to be confused with a put or call option, a stock option is usually issued to valued employees, allowing them to purchase shares of the company's stock at a predetermined price for a number of years into the future. Hopefully, when those options are exercised and the shares are purchased their market value at that time will be considerably higher than the exercise price.

stop-loss order an order to buy or sell a security at a limit price. When the market price reaches the limit price, your order becomes a market order and is executed on the next sale. You would place a stop-loss order to limit your loss on an investment. Suppose you purchased 100 shares of ABC Company common stock for $40 per share and you don't want to lose more than $4 per share or 10 percent of your investment; you would place a stop-loss order with your broker-dealer.

strike price   the exercise price of an option. If you own a call with a strike price of $50 and the stock is selling at $60, you can exercise the call (buying the stock at $50) and sell the stock into the open market at $60. The strike price is fixed and remains the same for the life of the option.

systematic risk   beyond the future prospects of the company itself to produce earnings, sell products, and become profitable, there exists market risk and interest rate risk. The company owned may do well internally, but interest rate changes and a falling stock market may bring its price down in spite of those profits.

taxable event   usually the sale of an asset at a gain or loss which would be used on that year's tax return; a realized gain or realized loss. The simple act of buying a security and holding on to it while it goes up in value represents a paper profit that isn't taxable since the gain was unrealized.

tax base   in the world of muni bonds, the tax base represents those entities in a community whose property taxes would pay the interest and ultimately the principal on bonds issued by the town, city, or political subdivision in question. A large residential or business population paying substantial taxes to a city makes it possible for that city to issue considerable amounts of debt, service that debt, and, because of the large tax base, pay a lower rate of interest to borrow those moneys.

tax-deferred   paying a tax that is due in a future tax year rather than the present one. Moneys working toward retirement in an IRA-type account, for example, grow tax-deferred and the taxes due are paid only when the dollars are withdrawn from the plan. A recently created type of retirement account, known as the Roth IRA allows the moneys to be put in after they have been taxed and then withdrawn tax-free when you retire.

term insurance   simple coverage that provides a death benefit and builds up no cash value. Term is usually the least expensive form of life insurance and can be bought in large amounts at a relatively cheap price to provide coverage for young, growing families.

12b-1 fees   fees deducted from a mutual fund's assets to compensate the mutual fund sponsor or broker-dealer for marketing the fund.

U.S. Treasury bills (T-bills)   Treasury securities that mature in periods up to one year.

U.S. Treasury bonds (T-bonds)   securities that are essentially a loan to the U.S. federal government, backed by the full faith and credit of the U.S. Treasury. Newly issued T-bonds mature in 10 to 30 years.

U.S. Treasury notes (T-notes)   Treasury securities that mature in 1 to 10 years.

unrealized gain   a gain in an asset that has not been taken by selling the asset off. You bought a stock at $50 and it is now worth $60. You have an unrealized gain in that holding of $10 and no tax is due until and if you sell. *See* **paper profit.**

unsystematic risk   risk from competition or obsolescence rather than from market forces or "interest rates." *See* **systematic risk.**

variable annuity   annuity in which the portfolio manager invests your dollars in instruments that can vary in value (there is a minimum rate of return).

venture capital   investment funds established to invest in relatively risky ventures such as start-up high technology or biotechnology businesses.

volatility   the rise or fall of a market, stock, or bond in a particular period of time. Highly volatile stocks are suitable for only those investors with a higher risk tolerance level.

warrant   a right, similar to an option, that is granted to the purchaser of a security. The warrant gives the holder the right to purchase additional shares of the company's common stock at a specified strike price at a point in the future, generally a relatively long period of time from the granting of the warrant. Warrants are issued in connection with a bond or stock offering.

whole-life   a type of insurance coverage that builds up a cash value from the premiums paid and the financial success of the insurance company, as opposed to term insurance, which provides only a death benefit. The cash value in a whole-life insurance policy can be borrowed out and repaid later, while such a feature isn't part of a term policy.

writer   the one who sells an option and stands ready to sell the stock in question, if a call option was written, or purchase the stock in question if a put option was written. The writer is often known as the grantor of the option.

yield   typically the return earned on a debt security. A $10,000 bond with a 5 percent coupon is said to have a nominal or stated yield of 5 percent or $500 per year. As the market price of that bond goes up or down the current yield moves in the opposite direction.

yield to maturity (YTM)   the average return on a bond between the date of purchase and the date the bond matures. This calculation takes into account the fixed interest paid every year as well as the gain or loss realized by holding the bond to maturity. Generally speaking, a bond bought at a discount and held to maturity has a YTM higher than the nominal or stated yield because a gain in value is realized along with the interest income (and vice versa for a bond bought at a premium.)

zero coupon bonds   bonds that pay no current coupon payments during their life, and are issued at a discount to face value or value at maturity.

Index